PLANNING THE CURRICULUM

for Pupils with Special Educational Needs

A Practical Guide

RICHARD BYERS
AND RICHARD ROSE

David Fulton Publishers
London

David Fulton Publishers Ltd
2 Barbon Close, London WC1N 3JX

First published in Great Britain by
David Fulton Publishers 1996
Reprinted 1997

Note: The right of the authors to be identified as the authors of their work has been asserted by them in accordance with the Copyright, Design and Patents Act 1988.

British Library Cataloguing in Publication Data

A catalogue record for this book is available from the British Library

ISBN 1-85346-387-6

Typeset by The Harrington Consultancy Ltd
Printed in Great Britain by Bell and Bain Ltd, Glasgow

Contents

Acknowledgements

We wish to dedicate this book to practitioners, with many thanks for affording us the privilege of sharing in your classroom processes and development tasks. The contents of this book belong, in many senses, to you, as you will recognise. Where examples and formats are taken directly from the work of particular schools, they are individually acknowledged in the text. We also acknowledge Durants School, Enfield; Dycorts School, Romford; Glenwood School, Dunstable; Grange School, Bedford; Heritage House School, Chesham; Hillcrest School, Dunstable; John Smeaton Community High School, Leeds; Lancaster School, Westcliff-on-Sea; Meldreth Manor School (SCOPE), Royston; Montacute School, Poole; Pen y Cwm School, Ebbw Vale; Rees Thomas School, Cambridge; Rutland House School (SCOPE), Nottingham; St. George's School, Peterborough; St. John's School, Bedford; Woodlands School, Chelmsford; the Northamptonshire Special Schools; and all the countless participants in staff development sessions provided by 'the two Richards' and other teams of teachers who have influenced our thinking over the past couple of years.

In addition, we wish to acknowledge the support of the University of Cambridge Institute of Education; the Centre for the Study of Special Education, Westminster College, Oxford; the Education Management Development Unit, University of Leicester; the School of Education, University of Birmingham; West Suffolk Professional Development Centre and Northamptonshire Inspection and Advisory Service. Thank you all, staff and students, for your interest and support.

Finally we thank a number of individuals for their contributions to this volume: Tom Rose, for assistance with computer management; David Banes, for ideas shared at the University of Cambridge Institute of Education Summer School; David Fulton, for continuing support and patience; and Chris Stevens, for his *Foreword*.

Richard Byers and Richard Rose, October, 1995.

Foreword

In 1988, I was a headteacher of a special school in the north of England. The day the National Curriculum Orders arrived on my desk I was convinced that there was a mistake and that they should have gone to the nearby secondary school! I waited for information on *our* National Curriculum, but all that arrived was a year of grace – special schools would have to implement the National Curriculum a year later than other schools. We decided not to wait a year but to start straightaway. Then *Curriculum Guidance 2, A Curriculum for All* was published in 1989 by the National Curriculum Council to support development work and further articulate the principle of entitlement for all.

Although we saw the opportunities for our pupils in the subject Orders, we also saw limitations. We felt, as further subject Orders arrived, that the framework emerging would cause us significant problems in accommodating areas of our whole curriculum. Something needed to be done.

The revised National Curriculum, September 1995, sets out a flexible framework which enables schools to plan their whole curriculum within a statement of minimum entitlement. How to plan whole curriculum coverage and teaching methods is for schools to decide. They can use all the flexibilities offered to tailor their plans to the needs of their pupils.

I welcome initiatives such as this book, by the two Richards, as a positive contribution in supporting schools' planning. There is no single right way to plan the curriculum. Judgements teachers make on how to ensure relevant curriculum coverage enable them to tailor content and contexts of the programmes of study to the abilities, strengths and needs of their pupils.

This book explores the questions teachers will need to ask in planning pupils' work and exemplifies some answers that schools have offered. It is practical, focuses on stages in planning, and guides people through a planned process. The book emphasises entitlement without losing sight of pupils' individual needs. It will help both schools who wish to review certain parts of their curricula and those who are undertaking more fundamental reviews of their provision.

Chris Stevens
School Curriculum and Assessment Authority
September, 1995.

The schemes of work process

These pages do not contain a neat formula for producing documents called schemes of work. We believe that curriculum development is a process entailing a commitment to continuous review and renewal. We do, it is true, argue for phased renewal, so that some of the stages of the development process we describe may produce outcomes which can be formalised into carefully presented long term documentation. We also make it clear that other aspects of the process must remain short term, subject to constant revision, the focus of hastily composed working papers and swift mental reactions, if they are truly to acknowledge changing priorities for individual pupils.

This book does not present a single answer to any of the questions it poses. Rather it calls upon the experiences of staff who work with pupils with special educational needs in a range of educational settings, all of whom make individual responses to a sense of common challenge. We cherish the diversity of these responses and have tried to represent as wide a range as we can in the following pages. We offer worked examples of sheets and, in many cases, blank formats which you can copy for your own use. You may find some ideas which you can pick up and use much as they are. We hope you will prefer to adapt before you adopt, tailoring ideas to the current state of curriculum development in your school.

We recognise that not all schools will wish to proceed from first principles. We have therefore designed this book for selective reading, with sections and sub-sections which are free-standing, but, we hope, usefully cross-referenced. The detailed contents page will help you find your way through the text. Our contention is that you may wish to start half way through the book now – but that you will need to come back to all its sections at some point in the curriculum development process in your school.

The schemes of work process

If you follow the sections of this book in sequence, you will move from a review of breadth and balance within the whole curriculum in section 2, taking account of practical timetabling considerations, to section 3, which is designed to contribute to policy making and review in relation both to National Curriculum subjects and other aspects of the whole curriculum.

Section 4 deals with the broad sweep of long term planning in relation to the programmes of study for the National Curriculum. We consider aspects which merit being taught in depth and those which schools may decide to cover in outline and draw a distinction between continuing work and discrete units of work. We explore the concepts of progression and continuity, through year groups and between departments, and advocate documentation which details aims, content and coverage in terms of programmes of study and key stages. We encourage schools to identify and capitalise upon the links between units of work in order to promote coherence. We do not consider it useful to prescribe a time period which may be considered 'long term'. Clearly, planning at this level deals with departments, key stages and year groups rather than days or weeks, but it is perhaps more helpful to think of this phase of the planning process as strategic, likely to lead to documents which are formalised and semi-permanent, the first stage in translating policy into practice.

Section 5 describes the formulation of medium term plans through units of work and modules which identify areas of work to be covered over a term or half a term. Here we suggest that subject focused content may be clarified by exemplifying activity at each age stage and that defining strands through sequences of proposed activity will enhance progression and continuity. Plans at this level may be formal but will be subject to more frequent review and revision than long term plans. They should also make clear the opportunities the units of work will present for continuous teacher assessment.

In section 6 we deal with short term planning and decisions to be made about activity detail on a session by session, week by week basis, at least during the development phase as staff build up a 'library' of teaching ideas. We discuss classroom processes and methods, including teaching approaches and learning styles, and planning for differentiation by accounting for a range of possible prior levels of pupil interest and achievement. We also discuss pupil groupings and resource issues concerning location, staffing, equipment and materials. We acknowledge that short term plans are likely to be informal, ephemeral, individual and subject to continuous revision in the light of circumstances during implementation. For experienced teachers they may also be more thought-through than written down, more jotted notes than typeset document.

Another aspect of short term planning involves target setting or establishing short term priorities for individual pupils. We suggest that these targets will be derived from annual aims or clusters of objectives and may be negotiated with pupils, parents and other professionals. Whether targets are expressed in terms of cross-curricular elements, subject specific skills, knowledge and understanding, or both, short term planning will ensure that opportunities for making records and assessments occur and are made use of.

In discussing ways of monitoring pupil responses, we emphasise the distinction between recording experience and achievement. We suggest that records should take account of planned outcomes and incidental responses, noting progress in relation to both individual targets and group activity. We explore, in section 7, methods of recording which are integral to teaching time, including pupil self recording, and acknowledge a range of sources of evidence, including examples of work, photographs and video.

Our contention in this book is that all development is cyclical and moves through planning and implementation phases towards a process of review and evaluation. This process operates on a number of levels. Teacher and pupil records will contribute to assessment and reporting and to the review of individual progress in relation to targets and priorities. Staff may thus use carefully managed sampling programmes to monitor the effectiveness of individual teaching programmes while information builds up for annual reporting, annual review and the recording of achievement.

In section 8, on curriculum co-ordination, we also highlight the importance of evaluating units of work themselves, ensuring, for example, that plans for assessment opportunities within particular activities are accurately linked to programmes of study and that work levels are appropriate, as part of the process of maintaining policy under regular review.

Figure 1:1 gives a one page summary of this process in note form.

The legislative position

Sir Ron Dearing's Review of the National Curriculum and its assessment (1993a; 1993b) considered and resolved a number of major issues. Individual subject review teams were asked to reduce content in what was, by common consent, an overloaded curriculum, without adding any new material. They were asked to clarify the essential knowledge, understanding and skills required in the National Curriculum by slimming down the programmes of study and reducing the number of attainment targets. The theoretical result of this slimming down is a release of time – at least 20% of the week, it is claimed, in Key Stages 1 to 3 and 40% in Key Stage 4 – which schools can use at their own discretion, perhaps devoting more time to aspects of the National Curriculum; perhaps attending to other priorities.

Part of the slimming process involved the rationalisation of overlap between subjects and the removal of references to methodology. In general, the programmes of study now no longer describe the 'how' of teaching – working in groups, for instance, – although this should not be seen as driving teaching in any particular methodological direction. We would argue that there is now an even greater need for teachers to consider and plan for a wide variety of approaches to teaching in order to encourage pupils to develop versatility in their repertoire of learning styles (Byers, 1994a; 1994b).

Neither has the process cancelled out the links between subjects – indeed, in many senses these are now stronger. Several of the review teams were at pains to point out the cross-curricular application of aspects of their subject – many facets of English, mathematical investigation and scientific enquiry are all given cross-curricular significance. The enhanced status of information technology – given a separate Order, almost a subject in its own right, but also mentioned as a recommended mode of access in the preamble to every other programme of study – also encourages cross-curricular planning, especially in Key Stages 1 and 2.

A drive towards consistency in presentation was also seen as an important part of strengthening the National Curriculum. All programmes of study are now subdivided into key stages under the standard prefix 'pupils should be taught to . . .'. Progression and continuity have been highlighted through improved 'stranding' in all the subjects and the scale of levels has been retained – with smoother progression between levels – to the end of Key Stage 3.

It may help to secure a positive approach to yet another round of curriculum development if staff note that schools are assured of a substantial period of stability in which the National Curriculum will remain in its present form.

Special educational needs The revisions outlined above may be seen to be of benefit to all, but the Dearing review paid particular attention to pupils with special educational needs. The introductory material in the revised Order for each subject contains a statement encouraging teachers to use appropriate aids, adaptations, systems and methods in order to facilitate access to the programmes of study for the National Curriculum for all pupils. It is the concepts which are important, whether these are accessed through signs, symbols, computers, sensory experiences, virtual reality – or, indeed, spoken or written language.

The changes go further. The revisions effectively uncouple chronological age from the notion of key stage. Review teams were asked to write programmes of study in such a way that pupils could demonstrate achievement at the earliest levels in all key stages. Where necessary, school staff are also given the discretion to teach pupils material from earlier (or later) key stages without recourse to formal modification or disapplication procedures, providing due consideration is given to age appropriate learning contexts. This means that a fourteen year old pupil with profound and multiple learning difficulties can be taught those aspects of the programmes of study for science at Key Stage 3 which are relevant and which can be rendered accessible while at the same time continuing to work on suitable material founded in the programmes of study for Key Stage 1. Stevens (1995) makes it clear that staff should look to the programmes of study devised for a pupil's chronological age *first* in their planning and that disapplication procedures must still be followed where it is deemed to be impossible to devise routes of access to an entire area of study, regardless of key stage.

Figure 1:2 gives an example of the kind of access statement which schools can now offer as a preamble to schemes of work documentation. This wording has been developed in an all-age school for pupils with severe and profound and multiple learning difficulties and it reflects the potential achievements of these pupils as perceived by the staff. The statement could be adapted for use in other settings.

Assessment In terms of assessment, the Dearing review resulted in a profound shift away from statements of attainment to level descriptions (with end of key stage descriptions in art, music and PE, where notions of 'levelness' are not seen as helpful). This should mean that tick-list driven teaching, focused solely on assessment outcomes, is no longer appropriate. As the *Introduction* to the consultation process (SCAA, 1994) states:

> . . . it is the programmes of study which should guide the planning, teaching and day-to-day assessment of pupils' work. The essential function of the level descriptions is to assist in the making of summary judgements about pupils' achievements as a basis for reporting at the end of a key stage. (page 6)

Commenting on how the level descriptions are to be used, the *Introduction* declares that teachers no longer need to apply a 'mechanical rule' to make complex calculations about scores in relation to individual fragments of achievement. Instead they should use their 'professional judgement', based on a range of forms of evidence, including samples of work and their own observations, in deciding which description the whole of a pupil's performance 'best fits' at the end of a key stage.

Closing comments

Taken together, these changes have resulted in greatly increased flexibility of access; wide discretionary powers for teachers and schools in planning activity which is relevant and meaningful to all pupils; and a rounded view of assessment with no further need for the mechanistic checking off of isolated performance indicators. These are profound changes indeed – changes which, as this book will explore, have particular resonance for pupils with special educational needs. We will therefore refer, throughout this book, to the revised National Curriculum (DfE, 1995) in all our examples and illustrations.

We hope that teachers, senior managers, subject co-ordinators and members of school support staff will be interested in this book and find its content practical and useful. It may also help governors, parents and other professionals who participate in the curriculum development process. We are confident that the ideas we present in the following sections will be applicable for pupils with a range of special educational needs, in special schools and in inclusive mainstream settings.

In writing this book we have deliberately sought to build on the ideas and practical approaches set out in previous volumes, *Redefining the Whole Curriculum for Pupils with Learning Difficulties*, (Sebba, Byers and Rose, 1993) and *Implementing the Whole Curriculum for Pupils with Learning Difficulties*, (Rose, Fergusson, Coles, Byers and Banes, 1994). We therefore follow similar conventions in attempting to avoid gender stereotyping and the unnecessary labelling of pupils. However, where the examples we offer relate to a specific group of pupils, we have, for the sake of clarity, identified them as having, for instance, moderate or profound and multiple learning difficulties. Readers should be aware that the precise definition of such categories will vary from school to school and from authority to authority. Our use of these terms should therefore be seen as a general guide to levels of access. We do, in any case, seek to broaden the debate where possible to emphasise the inclusion of a wide range of pupils who experience individual educational needs. We believe that the issues we raise in this book have relevance across that range of need and, indeed, beyond. The principles we wish to celebrate here are principles of good practice and it is not our intention to limit their application to any narrow or artificial section of the school population.

The Schemes of Work Process

Policy making

planning for the whole curriculum – implementation guidelines and review procedures

Long term planning

for continuing work and discrete units, showing aims, content and coverage in terms of programmes of study and key stages – indicating inter-subject links

Medium term planning

clarifying content by *exemplifying* activity at each age stage – showing sequence, progression and continuity by defining strands and assessment opportunities

Short term planning

of activity detail – session by session, week by week – showing:
- methods – teaching approaches and learning styles;
- pupil groupings;
- differentiation – range of possibilities;
- resources – location, staff, equipment, materials
  (a development task to build a 'library' of plans)

Short term target setting

priorities for individual pupils selected from individual annual aims/objectives (negotiated with pupils and parents?) expressed in terms of cross-curricular skills and/or subject specific skills, knowledge, understanding

Recording responses

planned and incidental, monitoring experience and achievement, noting progress in relation to individual targets and planned activity (samples of work, pupil self recording, photos, video etc.)

Evaluation and review

of individual targets and individual responses, activity plans, units and policy

Assessment and reporting

measuring progress against assessment opportunities linked to programmes of study and against individual aims/objectives building up information for annual reporting, Annual Review, Records of Achievement

Figure 1.1

Enabling Access

In the course of all schemes of work, this school will endeavour to maintain the conditions most likely to facilitate learning for all pupils through:

- the provision of appropriate information technology hardware, software and peripherals
- the correct use of positioning and mobility aids
- the observance of therapeutic regimes of all kinds – whether based in speech therapy, physiotherapy or medication
- the implementation of strategies to alleviate sensory impairments
- the consistent and sensitive application of programmes designed to moderate challenging behaviours

and through a commitment to interdisciplinary collaboration and partnership with parents, fellow professionals, pupils and the community of which we are a part.

Many of the teaching activities exemplified in these schemes of work derive from programmes of study for Key Stage 1. These activities have been carefully developed to provide continuity, progression and age appropriate learning contexts for pupils seeking achievement at the earliest levels across the age range.

Other activities are founded in programmes of study for Key Stages 2, 3 and 4 and offer pupils access to relevant, age appropriate material both at earlier levels and beyond. Some aspects of the programmes of study for the later key stages are liable to remain inaccessible or irrelevant for some pupils.

These schemes of work present a considered view of the breadth and depth of study appropriate to pupils at this school. However, individually targeted programmes are provided for all pupils, including those at either end of the spectrum of achievement.

Many pupils will need to revisit fresh interpretations of Key Stage 1 material throughout their school careers. For some, the challenge of achievement will prove problematic. In extreme cases, certain aspects of this work will remain inaccessible for particular pupils. In these instances, pupils' individual statements will reflect the situation.

There will be other pupils whose studies will lead them beyond the scope of the material represented in these schemes of work. In all such cases we offer individually differentiated enrichment activities, based on these schemes of work, upon other related aspects of the programmes of study for Key Stages 1, 2, 3 and 4, and upon other priorities within the whole curriculum.

Figure 1.2 Based on work done at Lancaster School

Establishing principles

The whole curriculum
The activities proposed in this section can be seen as a preparation for the work on policy making we present in section 3. They will lay some foundations for the long and medium term planning tasks we describe in sections 4 and 5. The discussion these activities will engender will also help to clarify a way forward for curriculum development teams already engaged in policy making and planning in relation to a range of aspects of the whole curriculum. The activities can be used to summarise and review work already undertaken and to set that work in the context of a revitalised debate about curriculum breadth and balance. *Planning the Curriculum at Key Stages 1 and 2* (SCAA, 1995) proposes a series of questions that schools might usefully ask.

◆ What must schools teach?

◆ What additional policies should schools develop which may lead to further teaching?

◆ What other areas does *this* school choose to cover?

◆ What particular curricular provision is suggested by the characteristic needs of the schools' pupils?

SCAA answers some of these questions by suggesting that statutory curricular provision includes the subjects of the National Curriculum, with associated end of key stage assessment, and religious education – aspects of the curriculum which are an entitlement for all. Areas where schools are required to have policy include special educational needs under the 1993 Education Act (DfE, 1993) and sex education.

Curricular provision about which schools choose to make policy includes the idea of extensions to the programmes of study for particular National Curriculum subjects – additional literacy work employing symbols, perhaps, or the breakdown of early mathematical thinking into notions of one-to-one correspondence or 'more' and 'less'. Other discretionary areas of the curriculum were identified in *Curriculum Guidance 3: The Whole Curriculum* (NCC, 1990a) as cross-curricular elements. These include the cross-curricular themes:

● economic and industrial understanding
● careers education and guidance
● health education
● education for citizenship
● environmental education

the cross-curricular skills:

● communication
● numeracy
● study
● problem solving
● personal and social
● information technology

and the cross-curricular dimensions, which encompass equal opportunities, preparation for life in a multi-cultural society and pupils' personal and social development.

Many commentators have since noted the particular significance of many of these ideas for pupils with learning difficulties (Ashdown, Carpenter and Bovair, 1991; NCC, 1992; Sebba, Byers and Rose, 1993). Others would argue that there are yet other aspects of the discretionary curriculum which are of particular relevance to pupils with special educational needs and which merit a place within the whole curriculum (Ouvry, 1991) – riding for the disabled, residential trips, lunch time clubs and community links might be examples of such ideas.

Individual schools will be aware that the characteristic special educational needs of particular pupil populations will generate further curricular priorities. These may include an emphasis upon literacy skills where significant numbers of pupils have English as a second home language; time devoted to physiotherapy for pupils with physical disabilities or to language and communication therapy where pupils have severe learning difficulties; or opportunities for counselling and guidance for pupils who experience emotional and behavioural difficulties.

The whole notion of individual pupil priorities is central to effective curriculum planning. The Code of Practice (DfE, 1994) emphasises the importance of the individual education plan, developed and monitored through the annual review procedure, for pupils with statements of special educational need. As has been clearly demonstrated (Ainscow, 1989; Sebba, Byers and Rose, 1993), schools need to balance the whole curriculum in response to pupils' individual needs.

Negotiating curriculum content

SCAA (1995) makes it clear that the National Curriculum is now properly seen as part of a 'broad statutory framework' within which schools are encouraged to 'create and pursue their own vision' (Tate, 1994). Curriculum development is once again part of the school development agenda (Byers and Rose, 1994).

Whether you are embarking on a review of the curriculum from first principles or pausing in an established process in order to take stock of progress so far, it may be useful to use the following activity to confirm or to renegotiate your school community's 'own vision' of curriculum content and to reappraise the ways in which your school timetable balances the complex demands of breadth and relevance.

Figures 2:1 and 2:2 can be copied onto card and cut up for use as a card game to promote whole staff debate about curriculum content. Governors and parents have joined in with this exercise enthusiastically and constructively. Some cards are already printed with the titles of various aspects of the whole curriculum – subjects, themes and cross-curricular skills – others are blank. Participants are dealt a mixed hand of printed and blank cards from a shuffled pack. Each player in turn selects a card from their hand and places it on the table, arguing a case for its inclusion in the school's whole curriculum. Players may comment about the role of each aspect and about the relationship between the ideas written on various cards. Comments and challenges from other players are to be welcomed.

Participants may swiftly decide that many of these aspects form part of the 'broad statutory framework' which Tate describes. They may move on to use the blank cards to make a case for including other aspects of the school's work within the whole curriculum as 'additional subjects', or particular school priorities. Players may call for extra sets of blank cards.

Schools catering for a broad age range of pupils will find that curriculum balance needs to be different in different departments or at different key stages. For younger children, for instance, exploratory play will be an important part of the curriculum

Figure 2:2

English	mathematics	science	information technology	art	history
geography	design and technology				
music	modern foreign language	physical education		religious education	
communication skills	numeracy skills	study skills		problem solving skills	
personal & social skills	information technology skills	economic & industrial understanding		careers education & guidance	
health education	education for citizenship	environmental education		sex education	

Figure 2:1

and for the under–fives, for whom the National Curriculum does not apply, other curriculum categories may have a major role to play. Ofsted (1995) identifies seven areas of learning for the under fives:

- aesthetic and creative
- physical
- moral and spiritual
- language and literacy
- mathematical
- scientific and technological
- human and social

At the other end of the spectrum, schools offering education for pupils with special educational needs post–sixteen will wish to consider a different range of priorities. Apart from those courses leading to qualifications, whether academic or vocational, Matthew Griffiths (1994) discusses four major aspects of the transition to adulthood. He argues that courses of further education must prepare students with learning difficulties for making decisions about a range of options in respect of:

- personal autonomy
- productive activity
- social interaction and community participation
- roles and relationships within partnerships and the family.

School staff working with pupils within various key stages or age-related departments may wish to come to their own conclusions about the characteristic balance of content which is appropriate for their particular pupils. The curriculum for pupils with social and communicative difficulties in year 5, for example, ought to be different from the curriculum offered to pupils with profound and multiple learning difficulties in their early teens. We would argue that this situation is made possible within the statutory framework and is actively promoted by the guidance.

Managing the whole curriculum

Having arrived at a set of preliminary responses to the question of what should be in the curriculum for various broad groupings of pupils at certain age-related stages in their school lives, schools will want to make decisions about how to manage these aspects of the curriculum and the relationships between them. We would argue that the whole curriculum for pupils with special educational needs is likely to be too complex to break down meaningfully into audited percentages of timetable time. A pupil with profound and multiple learning difficulties may be placed in her standing frame, and so receive a part of her physiotherapy programme, during a science lesson. A pupil on the autistic continuum may explore his feelings about his peer group, and so work towards one of his social development goals, during a class music session. Subtleties of this order will not be revealed in a simple audit of time allocation, especially since the precise nature of the balance within the whole curriculum must, we would argue, vary according to educational priorities for individual pupils as well as for groups of pupils in different age groups.

SCAA (1995) helpfully introduces a basic planning distinction between continuing work, which might be delivered in frequent, regular sessions or which permeates a range of different subject-related activities, and aspects of the curriculum which can be treated as separate, finite, distinct units of work. Staff may be encouraged to ask a series of questions about the aspects of the curriculum they identified in the previous activity:

◆ Which of these aspects require regular timetable slots?

◆ How frequent should these sessions be?

◆ Which aspects may be implemented in the course of other timetabled activities?

◆ Which aspects require occasional special arrangements?

◆ Which aspects should be seen as continuous, ongoing priorities?

◆ Which aspects can be treated as separate, discrete units of work?

◆ Are there links between certain aspects of the curriculum?

Figure 2:3 may be copied and used as a planning sheet enabling curriculum development committees, which may include parents, fellow professionals and governors, to respond to these and other questions about the management of the curriculum. Applying the planning questions proposed by Figure 2:3 to each aspect of the whole curriculum will lead departmental or key stage specific teams towards agreements about the characteristic content, balance, flavour and delivery style of the curriculum for pupils at different age stages. Figure 2:4 may be photocopied for use as a handout or overhead projector transparency in order to cue participants in to the kind of responses which might be appropriate.

Figure 2:5 gives a worked example of the timetable planner in use. Here a team of teachers working in Key Stage 3 of a school for pupils with moderate learning difficulties have made a series of decisions about the role of English in the whole curriculum for their department. They have decided to subsume the cross-curricular communication skills category in their planning for English and indicate that continuing work in speaking, listening and communicating permeates all school activity. They decide to run regular daily and weekly sessions, and give homework, in order to give due emphasis to basic literacy skills. They acknowledge that pupils will employ and generalise these skills, as well as having opportunities to engage with a variety of styles of text, in other regular sessions during the school week.

Turning to areas of the curriculum which can be treated as discrete units of work, they note the opportunities that pupils will have to read and write and conduct book-based research while studying modules in history and geography. They record their intention to access literature through a programme of discrete modules and note the outings, visits and special events which will support the study of English on an occasional basis.

This debate may well suggest that staff should cross-refer their intentions with members of planning teams for other subjects. This will ensure that the English component of history modules, for instance, is given proper emphasis and is duly recorded.

Although considering English and communication has encouraged this group of people to make an entry in each of the boxes on the planning form, there is no requirement to do this. Other aspects of the curriculum will not require such a comprehensive and complex response. Swimming, for instance, may only require entries in the 'regular sessions' slot, and in 'special events' if there is to be an annual swimming gala. Sex education may be treated as a component of science modules; a series of units in its own right; and as an understanding that pupils' need for occasional counselling may permeate school activities such as breaks, bus trips and residentials.

Moving on

Considering different aspects of the whole curriculum in this way will thus produce a variety of outcomes. Whole school, key stage or departmental teams will define the nature of the response they make for each aspect of the curriculum. The notes which are made should be retained. They will help schools to clarify the approach they wish to take in preparing to make policy and plans or in appraising progress in curriculum development to date.

Timetable planner:	area:	age:

Continuing work

permeating school activity *frequency – location – context*	regular sessions *frequency – location – context*	extensions to PoS in other subjects *frequency – location – context*

Discrete units of work

extensions to PoS in other subjects *frequency – location – context*	modules – units *frequency – location – context*	special events *frequency – location – context*

Figure 2.3

Timetable planner

area: *eg subject, theme, skill, dimension*

age: *eg key stage, department, year group*

Continuing work

identify
frequency – location – context
eg daily, weekly, in class, in community

permeating school activity
eg communication, sensory for PMLD

regular sessions
eg swimming, literacy skills, art

extensions to PoS in other subjects
eg cognitive/numeracy skills in maths

Discrete units of work

identify
frequency – location – context
eg daily, weekly, in class, in community

extensions to PoS in other subjects
eg sex ed in science

modules – units
eg 'The Romans', bridge building

special events
eg sports day, residential, work experience

Figure 2.4

Timetable planner: | **area:** English/communication skills | **age:** Key Stage 3

Continuing work

permeating school activity *frequency – location – context*	regular sessions *frequency – location – context*	extensions to PoS in other subjects *frequency – location – context*
Throughout school week all activities speaking, listening and communicating eg: questions and answers explaining, describing, narrating seeking information and support negotiating, debating, greeting nb audibility, clarity, grammar, turn taking	Class group activities daily practice in quiet reading, handwriting, spelling, punctuation, grammar, vocab. word processing weekly opportunities and homework in writing letters, lists, diaries reports, job applications etc. reading and creative writing	Reading and writing in most regular sessions eg maths, science, RE, IT and homework spelling, handwriting, reading – also look at styles of text, purposes of writing, function of text eg bible, modern and trad. scientific/technological language etc.

Discrete units of work

extensions to PoS in other subjects *frequency – location – context*	modules – units *frequency – location – context*	special events *frequency – location – context*
Modules in history and geography associated reading and writing eg stories/reports/accounts in history descriptions in geography; opportunities for word processing and noting variety of styles (handwritten artefacts, printed materials, other alphabets/grammars etc) use of dictionary/indexes and research methods – reading for info.	Literature modules plays poetry fiction reading aloud, listening, criticism performing, role play, improvisation character, plot, motivation style, range of media (video, film etc.) homework: creative writing and reading	Library trips to borrow & return books eg fortnightly Speaking, performing, reading in assembly eg termly Visits by poets, writers, performers eg occasional Theatre trip to see play eg annual Book Fair eg annual

Figure 2.5

Making and applying policy

In recent years, largely as a result of legislation, the development of policy has featured as a priority in many schools. Curriculum policies, special needs policies related to The Code of Practice (DfE, 1994) and others for aspects of school management have been established in most schools in all phases across the country. With one eye on the impending arrival of Ofsted (The Office for Standards in Education), schools have been concerned to put in place documentation which makes clear their philosophy and intentions, and this generally begins with the development of policy. If, however, the sole purpose of policy writing was to satisfy the requirements of agencies outside of school, it would be a thankless and largely futile task. Schools should defend their autonomy and their right to develop a philosophy which is unique to themselves. How often, in recent years, have schools hastened to adapt to new educational ideas only to find themselves forced to reconsider their position within a very short period of time. If policy has a purpose in school, it is in defining the individual characteristics which will enable the school to address most effectively the needs of its community - pupils, parents and staff (see section 2).

Curriculum policy should, above all, be about schools influencing their own practice, ensuring consistency of approach and, where necessary, improving curriculum delivery. Policies should further be regarded as a means of communicating the purpose of the school to those who have a vested interest – pupils, teachers, parents and the local community. The most effective policies are those which provide clear and unambiguous statements which can be easily interpreted and applied, and which can be used to have a direct influence upon the work of the school. Policies should be brief and should, of course, take account of legislation and reflect the ethos and philosophy of the school.

The relationship between school development planning and policy development

The development of schools is dependent upon the establishment of priorities which are defined by those most closely concerned with their management and work. Development implies improving practice, and moving from a current position where needs have been identified, to a new situation where changes made have a positive impact upon the school. Hargreaves and Hopkins (1991) state that

> Development planning is about creating a school culture which will support the planning and management of changes of many different kinds. School culture is difficult to define, but is best thought of as the procedures, values and expectations that guide people's behaviour within an organization. The school's culture is essentially 'the way we do things around here'. (pages 16–17)

The point made by Hargreaves and Hopkins is that each school is unique, and as such is likely to establish its own working practices which will differ from those adopted by other establishments. In recent years, schools have invested considerable time in developing techniques which have enabled them to define their own priorities, and writers such as Reid, Hopkins and Holly, 1987; Preedy, 1992; Southworth, 1993; and West-Burnham, 1994 have provided models and advice which have encouraged schools to develop plans for effective development.

It should be a matter of some concern that many schools are now reporting that their school development plans consist largely of priorities which have been provided by influences from outside of the school itself. The surfeit of legislation which has overtaken schools in the last ten years, has led to the agenda for educational development being taken away from those who have the greatest investment in ensuring school success. School development plans are too often concerned with ensuring that the requirements of outside agencies, such as Ofsted, are going to be met, and at times the needs of the school, as recognised by staff, governors and parents, are shelved in an effort to appease outside influences. Schools must regain control of their own destiny if staff are to be encouraged to tackle the important issues which relate directly to the needs of individual establishments. A tendency to regard the larger, national picture of education, as opposed to those matters which focus upon the school has, in some instances, resulted in the postponement of the very development which would enable staff to become more effective in addressing the needs of their own pupil population.

This does not, of course, mean that schools should not be addressing national issues. It has been argued (Byers and Rose, 1994), that those schools which maintain a principle of autonomy in the definition of priorities, also take on the added responsibility to ensure that in so doing, the entitlement of all pupils to a curriculum that is balanced, broad, relevant and well differentiated is not jeopardised. It does, however, suggest that schools should be establishing their own priorities through school development planning which gives equal credence to local and internal matters. Policy is undoubtedly important for many of the reasons outlined above. This section is concerned to provide a practical model for development which may be used to address a wide range of policies including those concerned with the curriculum.

A model for policy development

The relationship between policy and practice is an important one. It is through reference to policies that consistent practices should be achieved in schools. The notion that practice is wholly dependent upon policy is, however, a false one. In recent years it appears to have become fashionable to see policy as an essential driving force behind practice (see Figure 3:1).

Figure 3.1

Where this policy first approach has been adopted, it has in some instances resulted in schools rejecting much of their existing practices in an effort to redefine where they are going. There is a risk in this approach that good practice, possibly established over a number of years, can be devalued and replaced with an altogether less satisfactory situation. Even in those schools where there are no written policies, there is often an understanding of the way in which things are done. For example, a school may not have any written information about its lunchtime procedures, yet they may run smoothly, with all staff clear about their responsibilities, and actions to be taken. When considering the writing of policies, schools need to identify existing good practices, and to build upon these, rather than trying to reinvent the wheel. This does not imply that schools should completely reverse the above approach, as in Figure 3:2.

Figure 3.2

Writing policy simply on the basis of existing practice denies an opportunity to review that practice and to look for where it may be improved or modified. A more useful approach is to aim for a synthesis between policy and practice (see Figure 3:3) in which policy is seen as an opportunity to review and build upon good practice, whilst making amendments and changes where necessary.

Figure 3.3

There is one approach to the development of policy, not uncommon in schools, in which one person, often the head or deputy, is charged with the responsibility for writing a document, which is then distributed to staff for implementation. This does, of course, have certain advantages. Minimal time spent in discussion means that the policy is produced quickly, meetings are kept to a minimum, and it is easy to achieve a consistency of style. There are, however, many pitfalls. The policy writer needs to be precise in the writing, in order that all staff can interpret its meaning without difficulty. A lack of staff participation means that total ownership by all staff may not be easily achieved. It may also result in any staff who disagree with the content of the policy feeling resentment, and applying it only with reluctance. Worst of all, it ignores staff expertise and experiences, and does not provide opportunities for sharing in professional development.

An alternative approach is to involve all interested parties in policy development. This would seem to be ideal, but also has disadvantages and limitations. It is a lengthy and often difficult approach, and can make excessive demands upon an already busy staff. In a small school, staff may already be involved in several major projects, and have little time or inclination for attendance at additional meetings and researching other areas.

The model presented here provides a more effective approach which, whilst being consultative, also sets clear responsibilities and time lines. It accepts that there is a need to consult all interested parties and identifies times during the process when this consultation will take place. It also recognises policy development as a cyclical process, one in which the introduction of new ideas to the school, changes in legislation, or changes in the school population, can be recognised without a need for total reorganisation of the policy. The approach is based upon the cycle of development presented in Figure 3:4.

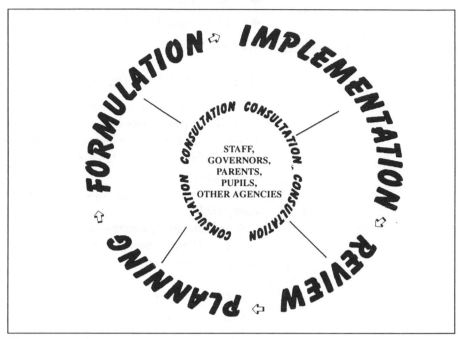

Figure 3.4 The policy development cycle

It should firstly be noted from this model, that policy development is not seen as a 'once and for ever' process. It is ongoing and recognises the need for review which will in turn lead to modifications. The model recognises that schools are constantly evolving establishments and that, as change occurs, there is a need to adapt policy and procedures in order to address new issues and needs. In this model, the process of consultation with staff, governors, parents, pupils and other agencies is protected at every stage. This model is central to the practical approach to be described here.

Using the model

During the process of policy development, a policy map (see Figure 3:5) is to be drawn up which will provide a school with an indication of the actions to be taken to complete the writing and implementation of a policy (Figure 3:10 gives a completed example). The headings at the top of the columns on the policy planning map are used to indicate responsibilities, actions to be taken, and time scale. The completed map is included here to give some indication of how it may look after each stage of completion. Please remember that this is only an example, and does not suggest the way in which your school should allocate tasks, or the time scale in which your school needs to work. The map must be used as a practical aid to development, and should not dictate working practices to a school. When the map is complete, staff should have a clear idea about responsibilities and the time scale for developing the policy. Only at this point should the school begin to follow the map through to its conclusion with the production and implementation of a policy. The map should be completed by working through the activities for the four stages.

◆ PLANNING

◆ FORMULATION

◆ IMPLEMENTATION

◆ REVIEW

Activity 1 The Planning Stage

This stage is concerned with establishing a purpose for the policy and identifying those persons who will be most closely concerned with its writing. It recognises the importance of consultation, by establishing clear roles and responsibilities not only for members of a working group, but also for those persons to be consulted.

As you work through this stage, the row marked **P** (planning) will be completed.

Complete this planning row by asking the questions at the head of the columns. Use the sheet provided (Figure 3:6) as a working sheet before entering details on your map.

(1) Where are we now ?

◆ Does the school have an existing policy in this area ?

◆ Which current practices do you wish to retain which may be contained within the policy ?

◆ Why have you decided that you need a policy?

(2) Where do we want to be?

◆ When you have a policy, what will be its purpose?

◆ Why have a written policy?

◆ How will the situation in school have been improved by the writing of a policy?

(3) What must we do?

◆ What methods will we deploy to construct our policy?

◆ How will we gather information?

◆ What guidance do we require from the school management? or the local authority?

◆ What do we need to find out about this area for development?

(4) What is the collective responsibility of people in the school community?

◆ What must staff, governors, parents, pupils, others do to help this process of development?

(5) What is my responsibility?

◆ If I have a direct role to play in the development of the policy, what will it be, and how can I help?

(6) How long will it take?

◆ What other things are happening in school at present, and during the immediate future?

◆ Do we have to time completion of this policy to coincide with a specific event? (e.g. a governors meeting)

◆ Which elements of the planning stage will take the greatest amount of time?

Time spent on the planning stage is critical and should avoid the necessity of redefining the working brief at later stages. During this stage, which is likely to involve a large number of people, concentrate only on planning. The greater detail of working practices can be established during the next stage, where fewer people are directly involved, and therefore the process may be completed more quickly.

Activity 2 The Formulation Stage

During this stage you will complete the row marked **F** (formulation) on the planning map. Use the sheet (Figure 3:7) to make notes before entering details on the map. As in the planning stage, you need to ask a number of questions which will enable you to enter details in the formulation stage boxes. It is likely that at this stage you will have a smaller number of people working directly on the task, and that you should therefore be able to make good progress.

(1) Where are we now?

◆ What has been decided about the way in which you will work?

◆ What brief has been established for the policy?

(2) Where do we want to be?

◆ At the end of policy development what will your policy look like?

◆ What will it contain?

(3) What must we do?

◆ How will we work to achieve the requirements?

◆ How will we consult with others?

◆ How will we disseminate any information?

◆ How will we increase our understanding of this area?

(4) What is the collective responsibility of people in the school community?

◆ Who has information which they must provide for the production of this policy?

◆ Who has ideas about its content?

◆ What needs to be read or examined?

(5) What is my responsibility?

◆ What can I do to assist this process?

◆ With whom should I consult?

◆ What information do I already have?

◆ What do I need to find out?

(6) How long will it take?

◆ What are the current commitments of the people involved at this stage?

◆ How often will people need to meet together?

◆ Which aspects of this stage will take the greatest amount of time?

◆ How will we make sure that everyone knows what the time scale of this stage is?

At the end of this exercise, it is essential that everyone concerned has access to the completed policy map, and is clear about roles, responsibilities and time scale.

The formulation stage indicates the actions which will be taken to write the policy. The next stage is concerned with putting the policy into practice.

Activity 3 The Implementation Stage

During this stage, you will complete the row marked **I** (implementation). Use the sheet (Figure 3:8) for making your notes before completing the map. This stage is concerned with what will happen when the policy has been written, and how you will ensure that it is put into practice.

(1) Where are we now?

At this point, you need to be clear that everyone concerned is familiar with the policy and its contents.

◆ Is the policy written in terms that are easily understood?

◆ Are sufficient copies available?

◆ Is the policy easily accessible to all who need to see it?

(2) Where do we want to be?

◆ How do we intend that this policy should be used?

◆ Is the purpose of the policy clear?

(3) What must we do?

◆ How will we disseminate information?

◆ Is there a need for training to ensure the implementation of the policy?

◆ Do we need to establish a system for monitoring the implementation of the policy?

(4) What is the collective responsibility of people in the school community?

◆ What needs are there for changes in existing practice?

◆ Who will read the policy?

22

◆ Are expectations made clear?

(5) What is my responsibility?

◆ Do I have to make changes to my practice?

◆ Can I assist others in the implementation of this policy?

◆ Can I identify my own training needs in relation to this policy?

(6) How long will it take?

◆ Will we implement this whole policy at once, or will we stagger its introduction?

◆ Are there resource implications which may affect the implementation of the policy?

◆ Do we need to take account of the time needed to train people prior to the implementation of the policy?

The final stage of this process is review. There is a danger that schools, in the euphoria of having written a policy and implemented it, then move on to another project without considering the importance of review. Policies need constant review, but it is probable that the first time it is reviewed after implementation may be critical in recognising success and fine tuning aspects of the policy which may not be as effective as they could be. Time spent in review is valuable, but must be accompanied by a willingness to make changes if needed. As a process, review should be constructively critical. Those who have been most closely associated with the writing of a policy will have invested time and hard work in its development. This is an opportunity for all charged with the responsibility of implementation to suggest improvements, but should not be seen as a time for criticising the writers. The policy map, if used as described, should have been the basis for consultation throughout and, by the time policy reaches implementation, should have done so on the basis of general consensus.

As with the other stages of the process, the six questions should be asked.

Activity 4 *The Review Stage*

As with the previous stages, there is a sheet (Figure 3:9) to help you with note making for this stage. During this stage you will complete the row marked **R** (review) on your policy map.

(1) Where are we now?

◆ Has the policy been fully implemented?

◆ Is everybody implementing it consistently?

◆ Are all aspects of the policy fully understood?

◆ Are there any obvious difficulties with the policy?

(2) Where do we want to be?

◆ Which aspects of the policy do we wish to change?

◆ What could make the policy more effective?

◆ Is there a need for anyone to change their role in relation to this policy?

◆ Are there further training needs?

(3) What must we do?

◆ Will we need to rewrite parts of the policy, or is it a matter of applying more consistently that which has already been written?

(4) What is the collective responsibility of people in the school community?

◆ What information is required from people?

◆ Who will collate the information, and how will it be used?

◆ Is there a need for any classroom observation?

◆ What information has been gained through monitoring?

(5) What is my responsibility?

◆ What information must I supply?

◆ Can I identify further training needs?

◆ Do I have a role to play in re-writing?

◆ Have I applied the new policy as was intended and agreed?

(6) How long will it take?

◆ Will we review the whole policy or one part of it?

◆ How much change is required?

◆ How does this review fit in to other aspects of the school's development at this time?

Once the review is completed (see Figure 3:10), it is then possible to use the questions from the planning section to assist in moving forward.

Policy should be used to assist schools in becoming more effective. As such they should be controlled by the school, and should not become the controlling influence of the school. The policy which does not have any influence upon practice is not worth the paper on which it is written. The model provided above should help to ensure that everyone involved with the school feels some ownership of the policy, but that it is developed in a structured, manageable way.

POLICY PLANNING MAP

School _____   **Policy** _____

	Where are we now?	Where do we want to be?	What must we do?	Collective responsibility?	My responsibility	Time Scale
P						
F						
I						
R						

Figure 3.5

POLICY PLANNING STAGE ACTIVITY

At the beginning of the policy planning stage, work together as a staff to complete this chart. When you have finished this task, use the information to complete the **PLANNING** line of your policy map.

WHY DO WE NEED THIS POLICY?	WHO WILL BE INVOLVED IN DEVELOPING THE POLICY, AND HOW?
WHAT DO WE WANT THE POLICY TO CONTAIN?	HOW MUCH TIME WILL IT TAKE?

Figure 3.6

POLICY FORMULATION STAGE ACTIVITY

When the planning stage of your policy map is completed, and you have established where you want to be, and assigned responsibilities, use this chart to provide information for the **FORMULATION** line of your policy map.

LIST THE CONTENTS OF THE DOCUMENT.

WHO WILL DO WHAT? HOW LONG WILL IT TAKE?

WHO AND HOW WILL WE CONSULT?

HOW WILL WE COMMUNICATE?

Figure 3.7

POLICY IMPLEMENTATION STAGE ACTIVITY

When the formulation stage of your policy planning is completed, you need to ensure that the work carried out is implemented by all staff. Answer the questions on this chart, then complete the **IMPLEMENTATION** section of your policy map.

WHO NEEDS TO KNOW ABOUT THE NEW POLICY? HOW WILL WE ENSURE THAT THE POLICY WE HAVE WRITTEN IS UNDERSTOOD?

WHEN WILL WE BEGIN APPLYING THE NEW POLICY?

HOW WILL WE KNOW IT IS BEING IMPLEMENTED?

Figure 3.8

POLICY REVIEW STAGE ACTIVITY

Having implemented your policy, you will need to review its effectiveness. Answer these questions before completing the **REVIEW** stage of your policy map.

WHAT QUESTIONS WILL THE POLICY REVIEW ASK?

WHAT METHODS WILL WE TAKE TO GATHER THE INFORMATION?

WHAT ACTIONS WILL WE TAKE FOLLOWING THE REVIEW?

Figure 3.9

POLICY PLANNING MAP

School *Waterside Primary* Policy *Maths*

	Where are we now?	Where do we want to be?	What must we do?	Collective responsibility?	My responsibility	Time Scale
P	No policy. Identified need to improve consistent teaching approaches	Clear guidelines for all staff. Information for parents and others. Shared vision.	Form a working group to include a governor. Conduct an audit of current practice. Review resources. Establish Inset needs.	Staff to contribute ideas and share current practice. Working party to meet weekly. All staff to read and comment on documents as produced.	To share my ideas. To attend meetings if requested. To catalogue my maths resources. To read and comment on documents at each stage.	Working group established by autumn half term. Audit to be finished by end of term.
F	Working group established and brief defined.	Policy in place with clear guidelines and agreement of staff.	Working group to meet weekly. Drafts to be circulated to staff for consultation. Final version to go to governors for ratification. Presentation to all staff.	Working group to give commitment to meetings. Each member to share ideas, and to consult with all staff. Writing of drafts and final policy	To consult with specific members of staff. To examine one area of current maths practice (shape and space) and report findings.	Group meeting weekly to produce draft by spring half term. Final policy by Easter. Ratification by governors at May meeting.
I	Policy available to all staff, and ratified by governors.	Policy being referred to consistently by all staff, and influencing practice of maths teaching. Policy understood by parents.	Implementation of policy to be monitored by members of the working group. Workshop session to present policy to parents.	All staff to read, and adjust practice to meet the requirements of the policy. Any problems to be brought to attention of working group.	To assist with monitoring. To ensure that my own practice is consistent with the policy.	Policy implemented in September. Workshops for staff and for parents during summer term.
R	Policy in practice and applied by all staff. Staff and parents clear about content and purpose.	Any needs for modification identified through practice to be noted and acted upon.	Questionnaire issued to all staff, and analysed by working group. Any modifications needed to be noted and acted upon.	Staff to notify any parts of policy which are problematic. All staff to complete questionnaires.	To help compile, distribute and collect questionnaires. To assist with any rewriting which may be necessary.	Review to be conducted during autumn term after summer implementation. Changes to be made before Christmas.

Figure 3.10

Long term planning

Breadth, balance and relevance . . .

. . . in the whole curriculum

Section 2 has clarified the statutory position regarding the discretion which schools can now exercise in their whole curriculum planning in order to ensure relevance. While breadth remains an entitlement, curricular balance may be seen as a flexible construct, changing from year to year, from pupil to pupil, in order to maintain a focus upon priority needs. Section 3 has given a practical means of translating whole curriculum debate into formal policy. Long term planning may then be used to control breadth and balance across the whole curriculum and within subjects. Long term plans should show, for instance, that an appropriate proportion of curriculum time is devoted to the aims and content of the core subjects of the National Curriculum while ensuring the place of other priorities for pupils with learning difficulties within the whole curriculum.

This may be achieved by means of curriculum maps, showing a framework of discrete units or modules in outline. Continuing aspects of the curriculum may then be taught either in the course of these units, as ongoing concerns integrated with unit content, or in separately timetabled sessions.

Many schools have already begun to address some of the difficulties of timetable planning by rotating some subjects within their plans. For example, a school may decide that an emphasis will be placed upon teaching an aspect of religious education during a particular term, providing coverage in depth on a regularly timetabled basis. In the following term, religious education may not be timetabled as a discrete subject, though opportunities to access elements of religious education within other subjects may be recognised. This sort of approach has certainly found favour with some schools when considering delivery of humanities subjects.

. . . within subjects

Long term plans also reveal decisions made about breadth and balance within subjects – whether enough time is devoted to 'shape, space and measures' in mathematics at Key Stage 3, for example, in relation to the work devoted to 'handling data'. It is the responsibility of subject co-ordinators, in dialogue with curriculum review teams (see section 9), to monitor balance within subjects at the long term planning stage.

Part of this task entails making decisions about aspects of subjects which are to be covered in depth and those which may be treated in outline. As Nicholas Tate states:

> At every key stage, there is far greater freedom within subjects to exemplify broad principles in different ways and to treat some topics in outline and others in depth. (Tate, 1994, page 19)

Chris Stevens stresses the significance of this discretionary flexibility for teachers working with pupils with special educational needs:

> These decisions on depth of coverage of aspects of the programmes of study are the key to ensuring that 'freed-up time' remains a reality for teachers of all pupils including those with SEN, and that the elements of the programmes of study which are essential to pupils' progress are taught appropriately. (Stevens, 1995, page 31)

Stevens goes on to emphasise that teachers should permit themselves to make 'professional judgements' as they implement the National Curriculum in order to ensure relevance in addition to breadth and balance. Long term plans will document these decisions. There will be no need to follow more formal routes to modification or disapplication unless, as Stevens points out, no attempt is to be made to cover parts of the programmes of study in any form (see section 1).

As staff make their long term plans, they will also begin to document and expand upon the decisions made about aspects of subjects which are to be treated as 'continuing' work or as discrete, 'blocked' units (see section 2). This fundamental distinction will also help staff to manage breadth, balance and relevance. It may, for instance, be important to ensure that aspects of the curriculum which are of crucial significance to pupils are taught continuously and in depth in regular sessions. Other, less essential, but nonetheless accessible, interesting, broadening aspects of the curriculum which pupils are entitled to experience, may be taught through a rolling programme of occasional topics or through single stand-alone units or modules.

It is important to realise that discussions about how subjects should be taught will not always lead to consistent conclusions. It may, for example, be appropriate to teach one part of the mathematics curriculum through a modular approach in one department and through integrated schemes of work in another. Using both approaches, over time, with the same group of pupils may also have a number of advantages. Employing a variety of approaches may mean that the learning needs of a greater number of pupils will be more precisely addressed (Byers, 1994a). It is clear that some pupils learn better in one situation than in another. Providing a balanced mix of styles of learning opportunities will also enable pupils to reinforce their learning by applying it in a range of contexts.

Continuing work

The cross-curricular skills

Although rates of individual progress may be variable, continuity between learning experiences should be seen as an entitlement for all. In many schools, the 'continuing' aspects of the curriculum, and in particular the cross-curricular skills (see section 2), are used to secure continuity for pupils across the curriculum and through year groups and key stages. This way of working can make it possible, for example, to ensure that:

- communication skills are seen as a priority for many pupils, whether they are in an English lesson, the swimming pool or the dining hall queue, and whether they are chronologically in Key Stage 1 or Key Stage 4;
- encouraging attention control is an important pre-requisite for some pupils

whatever the learning context;

- numeracy skills may be practised and extended in a range of situations across the curriculum.

Thus pupils work towards priority targets consistently in a range of learning contexts and pursue developmentally appropriate goals even as the age related content of lessons builds. It may be helpful to indicate this function of the cross-curricular skills within long term plans by summarising the range of typical possibilities under each of the skill headings. Figure 4:1 represents the response of one all-age school for pupils with severe learning difficulties. It should be noted that this is not a checklist nor an exhaustive audit of all the cross-curricular work undertaken by the school's pupils. It is, however, a useful statement reminding staff that all schemes of work have the potential for allowing pupils to pursue relevant, individual, cross-curricular targets (see section 6).

Continuing skills and processes in the subjects

It is also possible to generate similar statements delineating a range of continuing work founded in the programmes of study for specific subjects (see section 2). As SCAA (1995) notes, 'skills acquired in one subject or aspect of the curriculum can be applied or consolidated in another'. In the following example, Figure 4:2, staff at the same school for pupils with severe learning difficulties have set aside the continuing aspects, as they see them, of the programmes of study for science, geography and history at Key Stage 1. As we shall see later in this section, the schemes of work relating to the rolling programme of units at this school (see Figure 4:3) acknowledge links between these subjects. In this statement, an effort has been made to interpret and extend the language of the programmes of study in order to emphasise relevance and continuity with the school's particular curricular concerns. Although the schemes of work themselves acknowledge content from the later key stages, the statement about continuing skills and processes relates essentially to the programmes of study for Key Stage 1. This is because the school considers it probable that many pupils will continue to develop skills, knowledge and understanding at the earliest levels even as they engage with age-appropriate subject content as they grow older. In other circumstances, continuing work from the programmes of study for later key stages could be represented in such a statement, or separate statements prepared for different age groupings of pupils.

Much of the science represented here concerns experimental and investigative methods, which are acknowledged as having cross-curricular significance. There are also skills and processes with which pupils will engage whenever they are involved in historical enquiry or geographical investigation. Presenting the continuing aspects of particular programmes of study as statements within long term plans will also work for other subjects – for the general requirements for physical education, art or music, for instance. In many senses, this way of approaching the continuing aspects of the subjects will contribute significantly to the debate, and to policy making, about teaching approaches and learning styles and effective ways of promoting learning for pupils with special educational needs. Schools may wish to develop some of the ideas they identify as continuing aspects of subjects in more general 'access statements' about effective teaching approaches and learning styles.

However, these statements will not constitute detailed schemes of work from which staff can plan group sessions or individual objectives. Schools may wish to increase levels of detail for some subjects. Staff may produce extended programmes of study for the use and application of mathematics, or speaking and listening in English, constituting medium term plans (see section 5) reflecting work undertaken in regular timetable slots. Similarly, the development of information technology capability may merit detailed planning at the medium term level. It may require space on the timetable as a subject specific lesson in Key Stages 3 and 4 while being delivered continuously across the curriculum in Key Stages 1 and 2. Schools may wish to experiment with statements about continuing skills and processes while constructing long term plans for a range of subjects.

Discrete units of work

Where the continuing aspects of subjects are set aside in long term plans as discussed above, a task remains to deal with that material which can be treated as a series of discrete units of work. These discrete units may be developed as cycles of recurring topics, with pupils returning regularly to concepts presented in revised, age-appropriate contexts several times through a key stage or school career. This model works particularly well for younger pupils in relation to the programmes of study for Key Stages 1 and 2. Many senior schools opt to present a series of stand-alone modules of work so that pupils may only come across certain ideas once in the course of Key Stages 3 and 4. This section will examine both these strategies and the notion of links between units of work.

Inter-subject links and linked units of work

The process of establishing links between different but related aspects of subjects is not to be confused with strategies relating to the cross-curricular elements   aspects of the curriculum which may be said to permeate a wide range of teaching contexts regardless of subject content – nor the traditional 'topic' – in which a single theme was seen as a means of delivering aspects of many subjects. Traditional topic work has been subjected to consistent criticism over the years (Byers, 1992) but recently the concept of the 'subject focused topic' has gained credence.

Alexander, Rose and Woodhead (1992) put forward the case for a balance between 'subject and carefully focused topic work' in their report on *Curriculum Organisation and Classroom Practice in Primary Schools*. Ofsted, in their follow-up report (1993), argued that successful topics have 'a single subject bias or emphasise particular subjects.' National Curriculum Council (1993) described 'well-planned topic work' as being 'focused on a limited range of specific aspects' of the subjects but noted that 'curriculum coherence can be strengthened by linking together, where appropriate, units from different subjects'. Having received official blessing from Sir Ron Dearing in his *Interim Report* (1993a), this way of thinking went on to influence SCAA (1995) in the preparation of *Planning the Curriculum at Key Stages 1 and 2*.

This document makes it clear that linking units of work can be productive both because of 'common or complementary knowledge, understanding and skills' and because work in one area can provide 'a useful stimulus for work in another'. The document, like its predecessors, however, warns staff to:

● keep work focused by restricting the number of subjects or aspects of the curriculum to be linked;
● avoid contrived or artificial links between subjects or other aspects of the curriculum (SCAA, 1995, page 44)

and to ensure that any linking does not disrupt progression, balance or the separate integrity of individual subjects.

In summary, traditional whole school, whole curriculum 'topics' are not in favour although linking units of work can be productive. Schools should make their own decisions about when this is appropriate but be sure that links are carefully planned and constructive and that the progress pupils make in relation to subject specific knowledge, skills and understanding can be traced through linked units. Establishing sound inter-subject links can mean that learning opportunities become seamless, holistic, coherent experiences for pupils while teachers maintain a clear, unambiguous view of strands relating to specific subjects.

A rolling programme of linked units

It is now possible to look at several of these principles in action by looking in detail at the long term planning process in one school's experience. Having set aside the continuing aspects of their long term plans, the school in this example set out to organise the remaining aspects of science, geography and history in discrete units.

Returning to the programmes of study for Key Stage 1 of these subjects, the staff allowed the material to suggest its own groupings and connections. They identified the five broad categories of work which are represented in Figure 4:3. Some of this work remains subject specific. Unit 5, for instance, is concerned purely with science. Other units bring together linked ideas from two subjects – unit 3, for example, focuses on geographical and historical themes concerning family life, work and leisure. The five unit model, designed to be delivered over six terms in two years, allows for some Dearingesque 'freed-up' time. The spare term, it was felt, could either be used to offer extended study in depth based on a unit felt to offer particular relevance for a given year group (unit 1, on human development, was often mentioned as being worthy of additional time); or to revisit and revise aspects of the whole two-year cycle which had seemed to create problems for pupils, offering additional teaching and assessment opportunities; or to give teachers the freedom to develop work at their own discretion. The free term was, in any event, seen by teachers as a valued measure of their right to make professional decisions within a structure which might otherwise have seemed unduly prescriptive.

Having established a rolling two-year cycle of units, with space for teachers to exercise some discretion and to innovate, the staff took their thinking about the content of the units a little further. As has been noted, some links were already established. As the aims and content for each of the units were considered more carefully and title sheets for the medium term plans drawn up, it became apparent that the units would also offer opportunities for coverage of the cross-curricular themes – particularly for the older pupils (see section 5). These references were written into an aims, coverage and content statement for each unit, an example of which is presented in figure 4:4.

We will return to this school's work in section 5 in order to explore staff responses to the medium term level of planning and to the issue of ensuring progression through strands of study within these units of work. It is worth pausing, however, to consider an alternative response to the requirements of long term plans – and one that is perhaps well suited to the needs of older pupils working within Key Stages 3 and 4.

Making a map of stand-alone units

This approach depends upon creating a curriculum map by allocating individual units of work in particular subjects to particular terms in particular years. Mainstream schools are familiar with this way of conducting long term planning and it is a system recommended in non-statutory guidance.

Figure 4:5 gives an example of this planning technique in development. The teacher with subject co-ordination responsibility for history and geography in a school for senior age pupils with severe learning difficulties has begun to think about a programme of units of discrete work in Key Stage 3. She has referred to the programmes of study and checked the statutory requirements. She has set aside the continuing work in her subjects in process statements. After a departmental debate about whole curriculum balance (see section 2), she knows what time is available for her foundation subjects in the Key Stage 3 timetable.

As a result, she decides that history and geography will broadly alternate on the timetable. She plans to cover six units in each subject in the course of three years. Some units, she decides, suggest that links may be profitable.

The first unit in Year 7 is titled 'Roman Empire' and is a subject specific history unit. A unit on the geography of 'Modern Europe' follows in term 2. In term 3 of Year 7, history and geography are linked together in a joint unit on 'Native American Society' and 'Environment and Conservation'. The teacher feels that these two units of work complement one another and that there is common ground linking the subject content.

In Year 8, history and geography remain separate and subject specific. The two history units do not cover priority areas and will be covered in outline. The year-long project on 'Weather and Climate' will, however, be treated in depth. It will be illustrated by looking at the temperate climate of Britain (with opportunities for practical meteorological study through the autumn); continental winter in the Russian Federation; and tropical climate in the Indian sub-continent.

Year 9 is devoted to linked units. There will be a focus on an imperialist past in 'Britain 1750 – 1900' and the Asian theme from term 3 of Year 8 will be carried over into an examination of life in contemporary India and Pakistan. The final two terms of Year 9 give a chance to focus on 'Local Employment' in twentieth century Luton – an area of study which will be of direct relevance to the pupils and their families and which merits study in depth and breadth.

Having set up this programme of units, which offers coverage of the programmes of study and opportunities to study relevant material in depth, the teacher considers further links. She is already aware of the role which will be played within these units by continuing historical and geographical skills and processes – many of which will be founded in Key Stage 1 programmes of study and which will permit access at the earliest levels. For instance, the pupils will be able to make simple maps of the extent of Roman influence in Europe and compare these with maps of modern Europe. They will be able to make a time line showing Britain's involvement in India; the struggle for independence and subsequent partition; and the migrations which lent cultural diversity to Luton's community.

Beyond these links, which are within her own remit to establish, the teacher begins to consider the possible interplay between her subjects and other units in other subjects in Key Stage 3. She can immediately see ways in which her units could provide a stimulus for creative work and how art and music classes could support work in history and geography. She notes a range of ideas based on a variety of media and styles which she will need to discuss with the appropriate co-ordinators. She is aware that the English co-ordinator intends to experiment with teaching Shakespeare's *Julius Caesar* in Key Stage 3 and wonders if this could run alongside her unit on the Roman Empire. She finds other possible links between modern foreign language lessons and the study of Europe, and between religious education sessions and the study of different faith communities in contemporary Asia. Two further units suggest opportunities for accessing work from the cross-curricular themes of Careers and Environmental Education.

At this stage these suggestions are not final. They are simply notes of potential links which may become helpful, provided that planning across the whole Key Stage can be co-ordinated to take account of them and that the integrity of the subjects involved is not compromised. After due consideration and negotiation, an agreed version of the map of discrete units in Key Stage 3 will be drawn up.

Summary

Figure 4:6 may be photocopied and used to support this part of the planning process. It is important to note that single units may not always last for a whole term. Many schools plan units which run for half a term, or for two terms, or run two units concurrently in the same term. These sorts of decisions will emerge as the result of discussions about which aspects of the curriculum should be treated in depth and which in outline (Stevens, 1995). We explore this point in more detail in section 5. That section also addresses the issue of maintaining the integrity of individual subjects within linked units of work by planning for subject specific assessment opportunities.

Cross-curricular Skills
and
Schemes of Work

All activities will provide contexts in which pupils can apply, practise and develop transferable, cross–curricular skills. The range of skills will encompass:

- **communication skills** – from eye contact and interaction through the use of gesture, signs and symbols to speaking, listening, reading and writing;

- **numeracy skills** – from matching, sorting, grouping and sequencing through predicting, estimating, comparing and classifying to practical skills involving money, time and measurement;

- **study skills** – from attending, concentrating, and being willing to focus on task through skills in selecting and organising an environment or position in which to work to researching, managing time and collating information;

- **problem solving skills** – from an awareness of cause and effect through choice and decision making to investigative activities in which pupils learn from their experiences collaboratively;

- **personal and social skills** – from basic personal hygiene, feeding and dressing skills through to health education, home economics and self–organisation programmes;

- **information technology skills** – from the control of single switches, touch screens and concept keyboards through to word processing, data handling and keyboard skills;

- **perceptual skills** – from the perception of colour, pattern, shape, position, relationship and equivalence through to the making of fine judgements and measurements;

- **physical skills** – from skills of positioning and mobility through to fine and gross motor skills and hand–eye co-ordination.

Figure 4.1 From Lancaster School

Continuing Skills and Processes

All schemes of work in science, geography and history will provide contexts in which pupils will be encouraged to:

- use all their available senses to observe and explore at first hand;

- communicate awareness and understanding orally, visually, through role play, information technology and in writing;

- build scientific, geographical and historical vocabularies in words, gestures, signs or symbols;

- develop skills in sorting, grouping, comparing, classifying, sequencing and measuring;

- identify and describe similarities and differences;

- learn from stories, descriptions, eye witness reports, demonstrations, books, pictures, videos, tapes, television and information technology in addition to first hand experience;

- participate in processes involving investigation, exploration, enquiry, problem solving and group activity;

- use visits, fieldwork, practical activities, direct experience and everyday situations as starting points for enquiry;

- use sources, experiences and their own ideas in order to make discoveries, ask questions, promote ideas, test hypotheses and draw conclusions;

- obtain, respond to, select, store and retrieve information;

- report and interpret findings and data;

- record and present findings in a variety of ways, including pictures, diagrams, models, charts, actions, songs, speech, writing, signs, symbols, tapes, video and information technology;

- identify different ways of presenting ideas;

- relate ideas to evidence, finding connections and causal relationships between events;

- test predictions against evidence and generate explanations;

- recognise when tests or comparisons are unfair and when conclusions are not supported by evidence;

- acquire knowledge skills and understanding and relate their learning to everyday life and personal experience;

- follow instructions and directions and plan work independently;

- recognise and control hazards and risks;

- become aware of the passage of time and of the world beyond their own locality;

- consider how to treat living things and the environment with care and sensitivity.

Figure 4.2 From Lancaster School

Unit 2 – Plants, Animals, Weather and Climate

In this scheme of work, focusing upon science and geography, and environmental and careers education, pupils will be encouraged to learn about:

- plants and animals and the variety of life

- the needs of living things

- growth, movement, reproduction and life cycles

- taking responsibility for the care and welfare of living things and the environment

- working with plants and animals

- habitats and conservation

- making observations, measurements and recordings of local weather

- identifying and naming seasonal and global weather conditions

- the effects of weather patterns and weather regions on themselves, on other life forms and on the environment.

Figure 4.4 From Lancaster School

Continuing Unit
ongoing scientific, geographical and historical processes and cross-curricular skills

Unit 1 – Human Development
focusing on science and history, health education and education for citizenship

Unit 2 – Plants, Animals, Weather and Climate
focusing on science and geography, environmental education and careers education and guidance

Unit 3 – Family Life, Work and Leisure
focusing on history and geography, education for economic and industrial understanding, careers education and guidance and education for citizenship

Unit 4 – Places, Journeys and Transport
focusing on geography, history and science, environmental education and education for economic and industrial understanding

Unit 5 – Materials, Forces and Changes
focusing on science

Figure 4.3 From Lancaster School

Key Stage 3

Term:	History:	Geography:	Links with other subjects:
Y7 1	Roman Empire		English: *Julius Caesar* Art: *mosaic*
Y7 2		Modern Europe	MFL: *French module*
Y7 3	Native American......society	Environment & Conservation	Art: *wood, feather etc.* *Environmental Education*
Y8 1	Mediæval realms	WEATHER & CLIMATE (Britain)	Art: *tapestry/textiles* Music: *chant, modes*
Y8 2		Russian Fed.	Music: *Tchaikovsky*
Y8 3	UK 1500 – 1750	(Asia) &	Art: *clay/ceramics*
Y9 1	Britain.........1750 – 1900	Asia	Music: *classical & folk* RE: *multi-faith*
Y9 2	Twentieth ....Century ....World	Local Employment &	Music: *techno/bangra*
Y9 3		car industry in Luton	Art: *acrylics/plastics* Careers: *work experience*

Figure 4.5 With acknowledgements to Hillcrest School

Year	Subject:	Key Stage:
Term:	Unit title and summary of content:	Links with other subjects and cross-curricular elements:
1		
2		
3		

Figure 4.6

SECTION 5

Medium term planning

In practical terms, there may be overlap between long, medium and short term plans. In many schools, the kind of planning we describe in this section is seen as part of long term documentation – or, indeed, in other cases as an aspect of short term development. This is entirely appropriate. As we indicated in section 1, there is no set formula for the preparation of schemes of work and it is for individual schools to interpret the categories of planning we offer in the light of their own needs and priorities and to adapt the ideas we put forward for their own use.

What is clear, however, is that there is a task which lies between the stage of planning we described in section 4 – where broad aims and intentions with regard to content, coverage, continuity and links between subjects are set out over a time scale measured in key stages and year groups – and the processes we will elaborate in section 6 which are concerned with ensuring that individual pupils in particular classes have meaningful learning experiences day to day and week by week.

In accordance with National Curriculum terminology, (SCAA, 1995) we refer to this intermediate stage in the planning process as medium term. In many senses, however, the developments we detail in this section comprise the next logical steps in refining those formal documents which we have referred to as long term plans. There is no necessity to view the work we describe in this section as a separate part of what should be, in our view, a seamless process.

In section 4 we discussed the notion of curricular continuity in some detail. We now wish to turn to the parallel concept of progression.

Progression

Progression as differentiation

If the cross-curricular skills and processes which we identified as 'continuing' work lend coherence and continuity to the curriculum, it is the structured sequencing of experiences which can ensure that there is meaningful progression for pupils. A sense of progression through the continuing aspects of the curriculum has already been built into the process statements which we discussed in section 4. Planning for individual progression and achievement will be described in section 6. This section will explore the sequencing of experiences and opportunities within discrete units of work. Medium term planning will help to secure progress towards subject-related objectives and age-appropriate experiences for nominal groups of pupils at different age stages.

All pupils have a right to expect that learning experiences will be presented sequentially in a coherent way. Clearly, individual pupils will progress at different rates according to their interests, previous achievements and aptitudes for particular subjects (see sections 6 and 7). However, medium term plans for discrete units of work can be used to generate a framework which typifies and exemplifies progression for representative groups of pupils at various stages in their school careers.

Four kinds of progression

Staff may find it helpful to think about planning for progression in at least four senses:

- skill development –
  gaining new skills and/or maintaining, refining, consolidating and generalising existing skills;
- entitlement to content –
  extending access to knowledge and understanding into new areas as pupils grow older;
- learning contexts –
  ensuring that activities and attitudes are appropriate to pupils' ages and interests;
- functional application –
  moving away from adult dependence and classroom-based activity towards independence and practical, community-orientated activity.

In practice, these categories are inter-related and mutually supportive but they may help to clarify thinking.

Skill development

Progression in terms of skill development will be a familiar concept to anyone who has a background with pupils with learning difficulties. For many years the curriculum for these pupils was founded upon checklists of developmentally sequenced hierarchies of such skills. Whilst the teaching of skills in isolation is unlikely to be helpful for a pupil in terms of generalising learning, there is certainly a case to be made for anticipating skill requirements which will enable a pupil to make smooth progress through a lesson or series of lessons. Indeed, the National Curriculum proposes that it is important for pupils to gain skills related to specific subjects, often as a preparation for meaningful participation in more complex, investigative activity (Sebba, Byers and Rose, 1993).

In this book we have also examined the notion of cross-curricular skills which may be developed in a range of contexts across the curriculum (section 4). We have noted that it is possible for pupils to progress in terms of their communication skills whether they are in an English lesson, conducting a science experiment or riding a horse. Clearly, it is also important to expect and plan for progress in relation to subject specific skills, whether these are seen as part of the continuing work in a subject (see section 4) or as an objective within a discrete unit. There is clear progression in the programmes of study for music, for example, between making a record of compositions 'using symbols, where appropriate' (Key Stage 1) and using 'conventional staff notation and recording equipment' (Key Stage 4). This development of the skill of recording would be represented in units of work designed to give pupils opportunities to 'communicate musical ideas to others'.

We would also encourage staff to note that progression may not always mean that new skills are being developed. For some pupils, using an existing skill spontaneously, or consistently, or more confidently, or more fluently, or in an unfamiliar situation, or with new people may constitute very significant progress. Similarly, for other pupils, simply continuing to use a skill, or reactivating a previously established skill after a lapse in use, may be important evidence that regression is not taking place. Again, these achievements should have their place on the continuum of progression in terms of skill development.

Entitlement to new content

Even where pupils' achievements in terms of skill development remain focused on small increments of progress at the earliest levels, there is an entitlement to learn about new ideas as they grow older. In science, for instance, pupils in Key Stage 1 should be taught simply that 'humans move, feed, grow, use their senses and reproduce.' By the time these pupils are teenagers, with a legal entitlement to information and teaching about their sexuality (Scott, 1994), they should know about 'the physical and emotional changes that take place during adolescence'; about 'the menstrual cycle and fertilisation'; and about 'the human reproductive system' and foetal development. A comprehensive programme of personal and social education would probably also suggest that they should learn, among other things, about relationships, parenting and the right to choice and self determination in sexual behaviour in addition to knowing the stark facts of human reproduction.

Of course, creating access to this kind of awareness for pupils who, in terms of their skills and other areas of understanding, are still working on material based in the programmes of study for Key Stage 1 is a challenge. But it is a challenge which an entitlement curriculum requires us to meet. Units of work devised for older pupils will need to show routes of access to content which becomes an entitlement as a facet of progression.

Age-appropriate contexts

Thirdly, pupils have a right to expect that their learning, as they mature, will take place in age-appropriate contexts. Pupils may still need practice in how to 'recognise and use simple spelling patterns' (programmes of study for English, Key Stage 1) when they are fourteen. They should probably not, however, be exercising these competencies in writing a story about Flopsy-Wopsy Bunny and the Cuddly Kangaroo. The programmes of study for English at Key Stages 3 and 4 give a wide range of forms of writing which are age-appropriate ('diaries . . . personal letters . . . reports . . . reviews . . . newspaper articles . . .') and accessible at early levels of skill development, particularly in view of the statutory position on adaptations to modes of access (see section 1).

The notion of being age-appropriate should not become a dogma which leads to demeaning tokenism or stands in the way of work which is genuinely enjoyed by, and developmentally appropriate for, individual pupils. Nind and Hewett (1994) make a compelling case for continuing to provide intensive interaction, without regard to chronological age, for pupils who experience profound communicative difficulties. It makes no sense to deprive a pupil of a favourite programme of recorded music simply because it appears 'childish'. There is no rule which dictates that all teenagers will listen to the latest chart topping pop combo or, indeed, be dressed in the same adult interpretation of what constitutes young persons' fashion.

However, there is also a strong case to be made for designing schemes of work which broaden pupils' horizons and offer them access to an ever increasing range of options and experiences as they grow older. This may be especially true for pupils with learning difficulties who may not have other opportunities to engage with the culture of adolescence; who may be sheltered and protected from the world beyond home and school; and who may find emancipation from parents and childhood difficult to achieve (Griffiths, 1994).

Progress towards functional application

Emphasising the practical, functional application of skills learned in school is not simply part of the process of locating work in age-appropriate contexts. Encouraging pupils to put the skills they have learned in the classroom to use in the community entails more than a change of place. It also involves pupils in shedding their dependence upon staff support and adult consensus and engaging in independent, self-motivated activity. 'Following simple instructions to control risk to themselves' (programmes of study for design and technology, Key Stage 1) may be a reasonable expectation of a pupil wielding a hammer in the school workshop. Offering that same pupil a work experience placement making up fencing panels in a timber yard may involve risk taking of a totally different order, although this is presumably precisely where units of work in design and technology might be seen to lead for some pupils. Again, counting coins in class in order to 'learn multiplication and division facts relating to the 2s, 5s, 10s' (programmes of study for mathematics, Key Stage 1) will not fully prepare pupils for the complex demands of paying for goods at the supermarket checkout and counting the change. Well planned units of work can bring the practical application of school-based competencies into focus for staff and pupils alike and guide pupils progressively towards the goal of independence in the community.

Planning for progression in units of work

Returning to the long term plans for units of work we examined in section 4, it will be possible to see some of these principles in action as detail exemplifying strands of progression is built into medium term plans. Figure 4:4 showed an outline of the content for a unit of work about 'Plants, Animals, Weather and Climate' in an all-age school for pupils with severe learning difficulties. The curriculum development team in this school now set about designing separate but related extensions to the programmes of study for pupils in each of four distinct age stages (Figure 5:1).

The challenge is to pursue the strands (set in bold type) identified for this unit of work at the long term planning stage through each of the age stages (2 – 7, 7 – 11, 11 – 14, 14 – 19). Classroom activity, characteristic of each age stage and showing progression, is exemplified in italics, in the style of the National Curriculum programmes of study. While all of the work represented in this unit may be said to be founded in the Key Stage 1 programmes of study for science and geography (see section 4), the activities in each age stage build sequentially upon previous learning and introduce new skills, content, contexts and applications.

The strand dealing with 'weather and climate' shows clear progress in terms of skill development (Figure 5:1). While the youngest pupils use pictures of the weather to decide if it is cloudy or sunny today, the seven to eleven year olds use symbols to make bar charts as weather records. The pupils in the eleven to fourteen age stage move on to work with standard meteorological symbols and national weather maps while the oldest pupils note patterns in the weather forecasts in the media.

An entitlement to new content is reflected in this unit by the widening focus which takes pupils from a study of today's weather, outside the classroom window, in the early years towards an understanding of different climates around the world and their impact upon environmental issues globally (Figure 5:1, 'climatic effects'). Pupils could be said to have a right to understand about local water conservation measures as well as some of the origins of drought in the emerging countries of the world – both issues which they are likely to encounter in the course of watching television.

It should be stressed here that this matrix of exemplified activity does not require pupils to consolidate all the learning from one age stage before moving on to the next. As with the National Curriculum model, there is flexibility between stages and a notion that the work in the unit is cumulative. Thus it will be possible for pupils to continue to identify and name parts of animals (Figure 5:1, 'Life Cycles', age 2–7) when they are thirteen, but they might be encouraged to work on these concepts in the context of age appropriate experiences relating to animals at work (Figure 5:1, 'Life Cycles', age 14–19).

If this unit provides age appropriate contexts for developmentally appropriate activity, it also encourages progress towards functional application. The strand concerned with 'care, welfare and needs' (Figure 5:1) provides the youngest pupils with opportunities to identify the difference between plants and animals that are alive and items that are 'not alive'. In later years, other sessions will contribute to pupils' understandings about animals' food needs and about reproduction, giving access to aspects of the programmes of study for science in Key Stages 2 ('life processes, including nutrition') and 3 ('life processes, *eg reproduction*'). By the time pupils are sixteen, however, they may be learning to take independent responsibility for the care of animals as part of a work experience programme, thus integrating aspects of scientific and geographical study with their careers education and applying the skills they have learned in school to 'real world' situations.

It will be noted that activities relating to the cross-curricular themes become increasingly important for the older pupils in other strands of this unit. In fact, they lend a characteristic flavour of preparation for the world of work and adult life to the examples devised for students in the further education department in many of the units of work in this series (see Figure 4:3).

If schools wish to explore the notion of planning for progression by exemplifying activity, Figure 5:2 offers a blank format which can be used and adapted. This form is designed to cater for an all age school. In practice, many schools will wish to plan over two key stages rather than four and will wish to produce a two stage version of the sheet.

Figure 5:2 also offers age categories 'leading up to and including Key Stage 1' and 'including and following on from Key Stage 4'. Schools who wish to plan transitional curricula in more detail may prefer to experiment with the formats in Figure 5:3. Using these sheets, staff could explore the characteristic aspects of the early years and further education curricula identified in section 2 and their relationships with the school years. In doing so, staff will wish to consider the implications of their planning for teaching methods, institutional structures, staff attitudes, work with parents and inter-agency collaboration.

Schools may also wish to adapt these transitional planning sheets for use between junior and senior schools or between departments within schools, adding further refinements to planning for continuity and progression.

Assessment opportunities

A further aspect of planning in the medium term concerns projections about assessment opportunities. It will be particularly important to track progress in individual subjects through units of work where inter-subject links have been established and developed. In the examples we have seen so far in this section, the school has based its planning across a complex mix of subjects, themes and key stages. In setting down the opportunities for formative teacher assessment which the planned activities offer, it is possible to disentangle this complexity and provide clarity of subject focus and precision with regard to key stage. In this way, the units offer pupils meaningful, coherent, engaging activity which is not narrowly confined within subject boundaries. They offer teachers a way to maintain and complete clear and accurate records about the progress made by individual pupils through the programmes of study for particular subjects.

Figure 5:4 gives an example of how assessment opportunities may be written up and presented as an integral part of schemes of work documentation. This sheet refers back to the unit of work about 'Plants, Animals, Weather and Climate' presented in Figure 5:1 and contains a collection of relevant extracts from the programmes of study for the subjects and key stages which the unit is considered to cover. As we have seen in section 1, ongoing teacher assessment is conducted in relation to programmes of study. Staff will only need to use the level descriptions in preparing summative reports at the end of a key stage.

Schools working extensively with individual targets set in terms of the cross-curricular skills (see section 6) have found it useful to document the opportunities which implementing the programmes of study for the National Curriculum offers to make assessments of pupils' progress in these categories. Activities undertaken during a unit of science work can thus provide opportunities for pupils to solve problems, communicate or practise personal and social skills, for instance. An alternative way of presenting similar assessment opportunity material is put forward in the following paragraphs about the development of modules.

Modules

In recent years the use of subject focused modules has found favour in some schools (Rose, 1994). Special schools, and particularly those with a predominantly secondary population, have found them helpful in making full use of teacher expertise in specific subjects and ensuring continuity, progression, and full subject coverage. Some primary schools have found a modular approach useful for the delivery of a subject which does not easily fit into their customary planning methods. For example, some of the history study units, or aspects of religious education do not always lend themselves well to being assimilated into an integrated schemes of work, or topic approach. In such instances, it is often considered difficult to ensure that the subject is fully covered and that all pupils receive their full entitlement to the programmes of study.

For the school which intends developing a modular approach, a number of questions arise concerning format, and means of ensuring that the important aspects of assessment, continuity, and progression are addressed. These issues will be addressed in this section and working examples provided for teachers wishing to pursue this path.

What is a curriculum module?

A curriculum module defines the means by which the required content of part of a subject will be taught during a set period of time. It provides advice on teaching approaches, whilst recognising the importance of teacher autonomy, and ensures that the important elements of coverage and continuity are addressed. By developing a set format which is agreed by all staff, modules provide teachers with advice on activities to be undertaken, resources which may prove helpful, opportunities for assessment, and for cross curricular coverage. Effective modules ensure that each lesson builds upon the knowledge, skills and processes developed in the preceding lessons, and recognises that not all pupils will progress at the same rate, and that the achievements of pupils will vary. Strategies for differentiation (see section 6) are established within the modular structure, and consideration is given to means of providing appropriate access for pupils with special needs.

Effective modules should:

◆ Define the purpose of each lesson, and its relationship to the other lessons in the module.

In order to address continuity and progression, a module must consist of a series of interrelated lessons, each building upon the skills, knowledge and processes developed through the course of teaching. Progression will only be achieved if each lesson builds upon the work of those which preceded it, reinforcing the earlier work, as well as introducing new skills and concepts. A series of lessons, each related to a theme but ignoring the need for progression, will not assist pupils with special needs who need to develop ideas and reinforce learning over a period of time.

◆ Indicate activities to be undertaken through the module.

Modules take time to produce, but should ultimately be used to save teacher time in the future. If the intention is to produce a course which will be taught once, and then never used again, then it is probably not worth the effort of producing a module. With most schools now adopting cyclical models, and with much of the curriculum content defined by the National Curriculum, it is far more likely that courses developed this year will be used again in the future. This is where well produced modules have definite advantages. Teachers become familiar with the format in which the school produces its modules, and the indication of proven activities to be used with pupils, with a note of resource requirements, saves time in planning and preparation. The description of activities to be undertaken need not be comprehensive, but should rather be an indication of lesson content. It should be written in such a way that it does not inhibit individual teaching styles, whilst giving a clear path of progression through the lesson.

◆ Indicate opportunities for assessment.

Assessment should not be an 'add on' to teaching, but should rather build upon opportunities which exist in lessons for pupils to indicate what they have learned or achieved. When planning lessons, teachers should consider the assessment opportunities which they are creating, and should look for indicators of learning which do not involve the production of contrived procedures. In some lessons it is possible to identify numerous skills and a wide range of knowledge which could be assessed. Where this is the case, teachers should prioritise by examining the needs of pupils, and by addressing those skills, or that knowledge which will have greatest impact upon the overall pattern of a pupil's learning, and may be generalised to other curriculum areas. Assessment for its own sake has limited value. Effective assessment is used to plan further development of the pupil's learning. In the context of a modular approach, assessment should identify opportunities for learning within an activity which can then be built upon as the module progresses. The development of a set format which identifies what is to be assessed, how achievement will be identified, and how a pupil performed, is again a time saving factor which should be built in to the module.

◆ Indicate opportunities to provide access and differentiation for pupils with special needs.

Within each module lesson, teachers should plan, and indicate where there may be a need to provide specific means of access to activities for pupils with special needs. This will often refer to individual pupils, who may require specialist equipment, or positioning, or a means of communication which will enable them to participate more fully in a lesson. When writing modules, teachers may consider the production of additional materials to be contained alongside the lesson plans, such as worksheets, or self evaluation forms, which enable pupils to access a lesson at differing levels (see section 6).

◆ Provide cross-curricular references.

Even when working through a subject based approach, most lessons will provide opportunities for addressing the requirements of other subjects. Some indication of these when planning modules may encourage teachers to be aware of opportunities which could in some instances be overlooked. Producing lengthy lists of possible links to other subjects is not helpful as teachers will not have time to address these in any detail. Far more helpful is to indicate where lesson content will of necessity call upon knowledge or skills which may have been developed through other subjects, and which can be either put to practical use during the lesson, or reinforced through its content.

Module development in practice

To see how the development of curriculum modules can be undertaken in practice, examples have been included which should assist any school wishing to develop this approach.

Figure 5:5 is an example of a page from a science focused curriculum module. It describes an activity to be undertaken by a group of pupils as part of an overall theme of changes in materials (science AT3). In planning this lesson, the teacher has indicated the equipment which will be required, established opportunities for assessment, provided notes on access and differentiation, and indicated that a mathematical feature, handling data, is an essential part of the lesson. This format is an easy to use approach to module planning, (a blank for photocopying is included for use – Figure 5:6).

Figure 5:7 is an example of a worksheet produced to accompany the module lesson plan which we have just examined. Figure 5:8 provides another example, for a pupil who has more limited literacy skills. In this case, the worksheet makes use of *Writing with Symbols* (Widget, 1994). It is important to recognise that whilst both worksheets are valid, and relate to the lesson content, they are not dealing with entirely the same aspects of the lesson. This would not, of course, be unusual where the teacher was working with a group of varying needs. These worksheets, produced at the same time as the lesson plans, are contained within the module alongside the relevant lesson page. Further worksheets, aimed at specific groups of pupils, may be added over time as the module is repeatedly used as part of the school's cyclical approach.

Figure 5:9 is an assessment sheet which accompanies the lesson (again a blank is included for your use as Figure 5:10). This sheet refers to the assessment focus established for the lesson, with indicators for assessment opportunities, and a box to contain a simple statement about the achievements of the pupil.

As has been emphasised, continuity and progression are important elements in the development of a modular approach. Figure 5:11 shows how the lesson which follows the one examined builds upon the skills and knowledge developed. The emphasis upon assessment is the same as for the earlier lesson, providing an opportunity for the teacher to make observations upon retention of learning and consistency. Similarly, the worksheets (figures 5:12 and 5:13) follow an established format, but develop further the themes started in the earlier lesson.

The examples provided demonstrate one format for the development of a modular approach. Schools developing curriculum modules may adopt this format, or may wish to modify it to suit their own needs. The development of modules should be seen as a complementary approach to others described in this book, and is certainly one which may be considered for schools wishing to follow a more subject focused curriculum development path, perhaps one particularly suited to the needs and interests of older pupils. The advantages of a modular approach are:

◆ Plans show a clear path of progression through a course related to a subject.

◆ Classroom management is made easier through the clear indication of resource needs, and opportunities for assessment. Resources can be assembled before required, and then stored for future use the next time the module is to be taught.

◆ After the initial work in producing the module, course content is established which can be used and added to as required for future use.

◆ Staff, pupils, and parents quickly become familiar with a set format which provides a means of planning, and assessment which may then be easily incorporated into teacher records.

Breadth and balance

Whole curriculum

When medium term plans for units of work in any given term are brought together, they may reveal an imbalance between the subjects. As we saw in section 4, long term planning may involve an alternating focus upon non-core foundation subjects. This may mean that history is taught as a subject in the spring term, for example, but not in the summer, when a geography unit takes its turn in the implementation cycle. Of course, planning for the continuing aspects of the subjects (see section 4) may mean that historical skills and processes are brought into play in the course of this and other units. Schools should be confident that this is an acceptable position, provided that planning sheets and records show that there is an appropriate balance across a broad curriculum over time.

Within subjects

Section 4 also noted that planning for cycles of units or modules will entail making decisions about those aspects of subjects which may be treated in depth as against topics covered in outline (Tate, 1994; Stevens, 1995). At the medium term level of planning, teachers may wish to agree a commitment to cover the 'in-depth' material as a minimum requirement for all pupils, working consistently towards achievement and progress. Those aspects which are to be covered in outline may be seen as 'enrichment' activities. These may, indeed, offer opportunities for further achievement for some pupils who are able to move ahead but allow other pupils to continue to pursue basic skills and concepts in the context of new experiences.

Unit 2 – Plants, Animals, Weather and Climate

2 – 7	7 – 11	11 – 14	14 – 19
Variety of life Identifying and naming – domestic pets *eg cat, dog, fish, rabbit* – farm animals *eg cow, sheep, chicken, pig* – garden dwellers and mini–beasts *eg trees, flowers, worms, butterflies, ladybirds*	**Variety of life** Identifying and naming – zoo animals *eg lion, bear, giraffe, elephant* – wild animals *eg fox, mouse, pigeon, seagull* – local habitats and environments *eg woods, beaches, fields, rivers*	**Variety of life** Identifying, classifying and grouping by categories – of creatures *eg fish, birds, insects, mammals, reptiles, amphibians* – of vegetation *eg cactus/desert, tree/forest, grass/savanna* – of plants and animals in their habitats *eg birds/hedges, fish/sea*	**Variety of life** Evolution and extinction *eg origins of humanity, fossils, endangered species, dinosaurs* Ecology and conservation *eg rainforest, ponds, woodland, hedgerows, habitat destruction, pollution, resource management* Plants and animals in their habitats *eg waders/estuaries, frogs/ponds, dolphins/oceans*
Life cycles Identifying and naming parts – of animals *eg head, leg, ears, eyes, tail* – of plants *eg leaf, flower*	**Life cycles** Identifying and naming parts and characteristics – of animals *eg wings, beak, claws, paws, fins,* – of plants *eg roots, stems, petals, seeds*	**Life cycles** Reproduction, birth and death, life cycles – of animals, *eg eggs/chicks, spawn/frogs, caterpillar/butterfly, young/adult* – of plants *eg germination, growth, flowering, seeds, pollination*	**Life cycles** Animals at work *eg police dogs, carrier pigeons, horses* Animals for food and profit *eg poultry, eggs, milk, cheese, wool, bacon, meat* Exploitation of plant life *eg timber, paper, arable farming*
Care, welfare and needs Alive and not alive *eg animals and plants v. rocks and toys* Respect for living things *eg not hurting, not damaging*	**Care, welfare and needs** Movement, feeding, use of senses – in animals *eg food, water, warmth, shelter, exercise, response to sound/smell* – in plants *eg growing seeds, planting bulbs, water, response to light*	**Care, welfare and needs** Growth and reproduction – of animals *eg food chain, feeding young, milk, nests, burrows* – of plants *eg gardening, water cycle, fertilisers, soil enrichment, root feeding*	**Care, welfare and needs** Independent responsibility – for animals *eg feeding/grooming/walking the dog, stable/farm work experience* – for plants *eg house plants/window boxes/flower beds, horticultural work experience*

Figure 5.1a

Unit 2 – Plants, Animals, Weather and Climate

2 – 7	7 – 11	11 – 14	14 – 19
Weather and climate Identifying and naming local/seasonal weather conditions *eg sun, rain, wind, snow* Making daily weather records *eg 'Monday: today it is cloudy'* Using weather pictures *eg clouds, fog, frost*	**Weather and climate** Measuring temperature and spells of sun and rain *eg thermometer, clock, calendar readings* Maintaining weather charts over time *eg rain, sun, temperature and daylength* Using graphs and symbols *eg cloud, raindrop, sun, bar charts*	**Weather and climate** Using a weather station *eg wind speed, wind direction, rainfall* Recording local weather *eg prevailing winds, rainfall patterns* Recognising standard meteorological symbols *eg national weather maps*	**Weather and climate** Safety precautions *eg frost, gales, ice. lightning, sunburn* Interpretation and use of weather forecasts *eg frost, wind damage, flood, sun, planning an outing* Use of standard forecasts *eg newspaper, TV*
Climatic effects Naming weather conditions and sensory effects *eg hot, cold, wet, dry* Naming the seasons *eg spring, summer, autumn, winter*	**Climatic effects** Seasonal weather effects *eg clothes for keeping warm/dry, growth in spring/leaf fall in autumn* Sequencing the seasons *eg months of the year, summer holidays, harvest*	**Climatic effects** Local weather effects *eg wind damage, garden waterlogged, shade and shelter* World climate *eg rainforest, desert, tropics, arctic*	**Climatic effects** Global weather effects *eg drought, flood, crop failure* Environmental issues *eg desertification, water conservation, ozone depletion, global warming, acid rain*

Figure 5.1b From Lancaster School

Unit: **Title:**

PROGRAMME of STUDY FOCUS:
with links into:

Key Stage 1 Activities	Key Stage 2 Activities	Key Stage 3 Activities	Key Stage 4 Activities

Figure 5.2

Further Education – Curriculum Framework

School work in preparation for FE	School work continued into FE	New experiences specific to FE

Early Years – Curriculum Framework

New experiences specific to Early Years	Preparation for School in Early Years work	Early Years work continued into School

Figure 5.3

Lancaster School Integrated Scheme of Work
Animals, Plants, Weather and Climate. National Curriculum references:

In covering this unit pupils may demonstrate progress towards learning the following:

Science
Key Stage 1   Pupils should be given opportunities to:
2 Science in   a relate their understanding of science to domestic and environmental contexts;
  everyday life   b consider ways in which science is relevant to their personal health;
                           c consider how to treat living things and the environment with care and sensitivity.
                              Pupils should be taught to:
4 Communication   a use scientific vocabulary to name and describe living things, materials, phenomena and
                              processes;
5 Health and safety   a recognise hazards and risks when working with living things and materials;
                           b follow simple instructions to control the risks to themselves.
2 Obtaining evidence   a to explore using appropriate senses;
                              Pupils should be taught:
1 Life processes   a the differences between things that are living and things that have never been alive;
                           b that animals, including humans, move, feed, grow, use their senses and reproduce.
3 Green plants as   a that plants need light and water to grow;
  organisms   b to recognise and name the leaf, flower, stem and root of flowering plants;
                           c that flowering plants grow and produce seeds which, in turn, produce new plants.
4 Variation and
  classification   b that living things can be grouped according to observable similarities and differences.
5 Living things in   a that there are different kinds of plants and animals in the local environment.
  their environment   b that there are differences between local environments and that these affect which animals and
                              plants are found there.

Science
Key Stage 2   Pupils should be taught:
1 Life processes   a that there are life processes, including nutrition, movement, growth and reproduction,
                              common to animals, including humans;
                           b that there are life processes, including growth, nutrition and reproduction, common to plants.

3 Green plants as
  organisms
growth and nutrition   a that plant growth is affected by the availability of light and water, and by temperature;
                           b that plants need light to produce food for growth, and the importance of the leaf in this
                              process;
                           c that the root anchors the plant, and that water and nutrients are taken in through the root and
                              transported through the stem to other parts of the plant;
reproduction   d about the life cycle of flowering plants, including pollination, seed production, seed dispersal,
                              reproduction and germination.
4 Variation and   a how locally occurring animals and plants can be identified and assigned to groups,
  classification   using keys.

5 Living things in
  their environment
  adaptation   a that different plants and animals are found in different habitats;
                           b how animals and plants in two different habitats are suited to their environment;
feeding relationships c that food chains show feeding relationships in an ecosystem;
                           d that nearly all food chains start with a green plant;
micro-organisms   e that micro-organisms exist, and that many may be beneficial, *eg in the breakdown of waste*,
                              while others may be harmful, *eg in causing disease*

Geography
Key Stage 1   In these studies, pupils should be taught:
5   c about the effects of weather on people and their surroundings, *eg the effect of seasonal
                              variations in temperature on the clothes people wear.*

Geography
Key Stage 2
3   a use appropriate geographical vocabulary, *eg temperature, transport, industry, agriculture,* to
                              describe and interpret their surroundings.
8 Weather   In studying how weather varies between places and over time, pupils should be taught:
                           a how site conditions can influence the weather, *eg temperatures in the shade and in the sun,
                              wind speed in sheltered and exposed sites;*
                           b about seasonal weather patterns;
                           c about weather conditions in different parts of the world, *eg temperatures, rainfall and sunshine
                              conditions in the localities studied, extremes of weather in other parts of the world.*

Figure 5.4 Lancaster School

CURRICULUM MODULE TITLE: Changes in materials (SCIENCE AT3.)
Lesson number 5 Ice cubes and insulation (1)

Equipment

Activities

Focus for assessment

Access/differentiation

Cross curricular references

Figure 5.5

Changes in materials lesson 5
Ice cubes and insulation

Where did you put your 4 ice cubes?

Ice cube 1

Ice cube 2

Ice cube 3

Ice cube 4

Which one did you think would be the slowest to melt?

How long did you think it would take to melt?

How long did it take to melt?

Which one did you think would be the quickest to melt?

How long did you think it would take to melt?

How long did it take to melt?

Write a few sentences about the changes to the ice cubes which took place.

Figure 5.7

CURRICULUM MODULE TITLE: Changes in materials (SCIENCE AT3.)
Lesson number 5 Ice cubes and insulation (1)

Equipment
Ice cubes, jars for the cubes, worksheets and pencils.

Activities
Pupils to place ice cubes in a variety of locations, and to predict the time it will take for them to melt completely.

Pupil's to choose locations, and to predict which will be the quickest to melt, and which the slowest, and to give approximate times.

Discuss reasons for pupil's predictions. Note what changes are involved, and what factors influence the rate of change.

Record results and complete worksheets.

Focus for assessment
Pupil's abilities in prediction.
Observation of change.

Access/differentiation
Two levels of worksheet
Some pupils to record results using stopwatches, others to use terms such as longest time, and shortest time without using standard measures.

Cross curricular references
Mathematics – Handling data

Figure 5.6

Changes in materials lesson 5
Ice cubes and insulation (1)
Assessment Sheet

Pupil's name   **date**

Assessment focus
Pupil's ability to make predictions

Indicators
Pupil contributes predictions about which ice cubes will melt quickest, slowest, during discussion.
Predictions accompanied by reasoning. – e.g. the ice cubes on the window ledge will melt quickly because of the heat from the sun.
Evidence through answers given on worksheets.

Assessment statement
_____ was/was not able to make predictions based upon reasoning during the lesson.

Assessment focus
Pupil's skills in observing change

Indicators
A   Pupil able to indicate that ice cubes changed gradually from a solid state (ice), through a process of melting to a liquid state (water).
B   Pupil able to indicate the effects which different locations had upon the time which it took for ice cubes to melt.
Evidence through discussion, and through worksheets.

Assessment statement
_____ was/was not able to observe changes to the ice cubes.
_____ was/was not able to indicate the influence of different locations upon the ice cubes.

Figure 5.9

Changes in materials lesson 5
Ice cubes and insulation

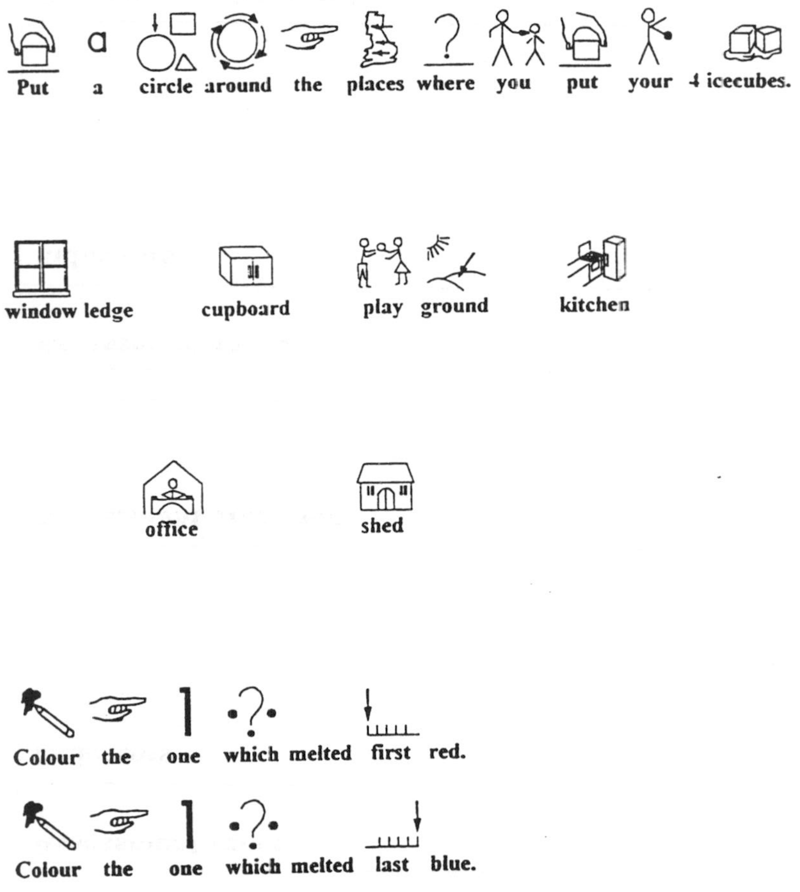

Put a circle around the places where you put your 4 icecubes.

window ledge   cupboard   play ground   kitchen

office   shed

Colour the one which melted first red.

Colour the one which melted last blue.

Figure 5.8

55

Module Assessment Sheet

Pupil's name   **date**

Assessment focus

Indicators

Assessment statement

Assessment focus

Indicators

Assessment statement

Figure 5.10

CURRICULUM MODULE TITLE:

Changes in materials (SCIENCE AT3.)

Lesson number 6 Ice cubes and insulation (2)

Equipment

Ice cubes, jars for ice cubes, range of materials for insulation, including plastic, newspaper, cartridge paper, cloth (three different types), polystyrene. Scissors, worksheets, pencils, sticky tape, glue sticks.

Activities

Pupils to devise methods to make ice cubes melt more slowly in the same locations as used previously.
Discuss concept of a fair test with pupils, temperature in locations today may differ from last week.
Provide pupils with a range of materials to use, and encourage them to make predictions about insulation properties of these materials.
Use worksheets and produce charts to record results.

Focus for assessment

Pupil's abilities in prediction.

Access/differentiation

Two levels of worksheet
Pupils to work in groups, with support given to pupils who have difficulties cutting materials. Classroom assistant to talk through last week's lesson with pupils who have difficulties retaining information.

Cross curricular references

Mathematics – Handling date

Figure 5.11

Changes in materials lesson 6
Ice cubes and insulation

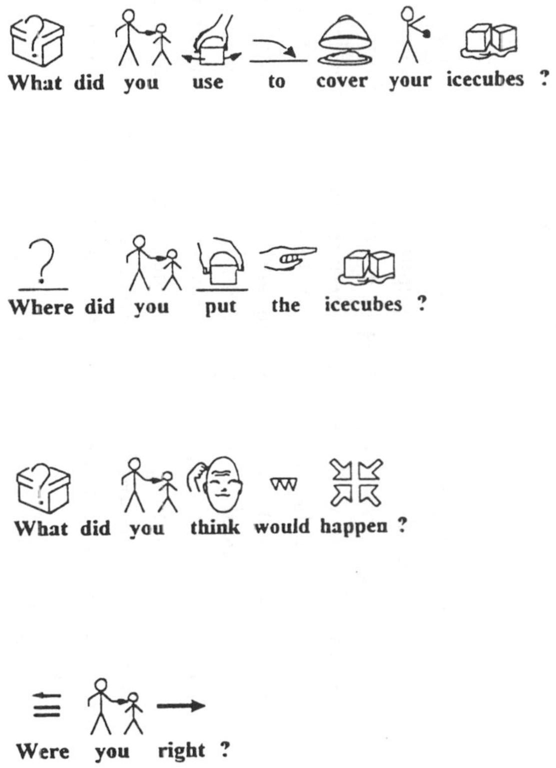

What did you use to cover your icecubes ?

Where did you put the icecubes ?

What did you think would happen ?

Were you right ?

Figure 5.13

Changes in materials lesson 6
Ice cubes and insulation

Which material did you think would work best as an insulator?

Why did you think this would work best?

Were you right?

How long did it take for the ice cube to melt?

Find your sheet from last week. How long did the ice cube in the same place take to melt last week?

Can you think of anywhere in your home where insulation is used?

Figure 5.12

Short term planning

Short term planning may occur both in relation to group activity and to learning priorities for individual pupils. We would argue that detailed short term lesson or activity planning in a written form is not necessary for every session of every week, especially where teachers are experienced with both the subject matter they are covering and the pupil group they are teaching. Under these circumstances, the reworking and adaptation of tried and tested activity plans to the needs of a new year group of pupils may be an informal, internal, largely cerebral process. Indeed, we would argue that attention paid to formal short term planning in the development phase, and the adoption of selected, well-constituted specimen activity plans as exemplary materials within schemes of work documentation, means that staff will not have to re-invent the wheel constantly.

On the other hand, staff should not expect to be able to work from a standard syllabus year after year, term by term. Short term planning in respect of pupils' changing individual needs and those precise strategies which will ensure access to the curriculum and achievement in response to learning opportunities should be seen as an ongoing requirement for all staff working with pupils with special educational needs.

Activity planning

As Sebba (1994) suggests, subject specialist teachers, subject co-ordinators, and, indeed, other interested and enthusiastic members of staff will generate a 'resource bank' of activity plans as they implement the units of work agreed upon during the long and medium term planning phases. It will be useful to make a point of writing up and collating a range of these specimen plans as units of work are developed and implemented and to add to this collection as experience and evaluation indicates improvements, amendments or additions to the resource bank. We contend that such activity plans should not be seen as prescriptive or exclusively the 'right' way to approach aspects of teaching, but should be presented, in a spirit of shared expertise and support, as useful ideas which have worked well in the past and which might be used as a stimulus for further development. They may be appended behind medium term plans in schemes of work documentation and maintained under review as a portfolio of specimen solutions to the challenge of implementation (see section 5).

Short term plans may help staff to focus their thinking on a wide range of issues, in particular, how to:

- ensure meaningful access routes to curriculum content by generating extensions to the programmes of study;
- differentiate activities successfully for a representative range of pupils;

- create a balance between experiential, investigative styles of learning, routine acquisition and maintenance of skills and activities which allow pupils to assimilate, consolidate or apply new understandings;
- integrate cross-curricular elements successfully in subject focused teaching;
- plan for pupil collaboration and co-operative group work in balance with individual work and class activity;
- select appropriate resources and use them to best advantage in relation to specific aspects of a unit of work;
- manage time, staff, volunteers, equipment and space to the benefit of pupils and their learning;
- create opportunities to record achievement and assess pupil progress against individual targets and in relation to subject specific aims.

Many experienced teachers, when planning work for new, unfamiliar groups of pupils, or coming to terms with subject content new to them, or when freshening up previously taught aspects of units of work in the light of evaluation, will want to continue to plan certain activities in some detail. Often such activity will be the 'set piece' which provides the focus for a sequence of related, more routine, activities – a site visit, perhaps, or an in-school simulation; a major practical investigation or a dramatic presentation as the culmination of a series of related sessions. There is no doubt that such selective planning will also enhance teaching and learning during the satellite sessions which enable pupils to prepare for and follow through the experiences gained during well-planned, central activity.

Some examples may serve to illustrate the issues. Figure 6:1 shows a lesson planning sheet which allows the teacher to prepare for a single science lesson – one of a series of such sessions outlined in medium term plans for units of work (see section 5). She considers pupil groupings and broadly differentiated activity (see below in this section). She thinks about how she means to deploy staff and volunteers and she makes a note of the resources she will require for the lesson. She uses the final section of the sheet to make notes about outcomes for individual pupils and may use these data to evaluate the effectiveness of her teaching; to reconsider the pupil groupings she has set up; and to monitor pupil progress and achievement (see section 7).

In Figure 6:2 we find a number of similar features, although this is a plan for a series of physical education sessions for a particular class of pupils. Again, groups are established and attention is paid to aims and objectives as well as to plans for activity linked to assessment opportunities (see section 5). As well as noting the resources she will need, this teacher makes notes about the records she wishes to keep in relation to these sessions and, after the event, makes evaluative comments which may feed into her planning for future sessions. It is worth remarking that the general sections of a sheet like this (aims, assessment opportunities, resources and recording) could be filled and copied in order that the particular sections can be tailored for use with different groups.

Figure 6:3 also shows a plan for a half term series of history lessons in Key Stage 3. This teacher again records the aims of the sessions, as key concepts to be studied, and notes the resources required. This sheet then charts the difference between planned activity, in the left hand column, and what the pupils actually experienced, on the right. At first things proceed more or less according to plan, with the teacher noting particular aspects which have caught the pupils' imaginations (Latin names and Roman coins, for instance), but the blanket dig, where pupils lift layers of blankets and 'unearth' ever older items as they move down through the layers, proves to be such an exciting activity in its own right that the planned recording is not carried out. This work is completed the following week back at school and the plaster casting is postponed for another session. These notes, taken alongside records of the responses of individual pupils will constitute both a valuable record of experience for this whole class (see section 7) and a means of evaluating the unit of work when the time comes to teach this study unit again.

We will now turn to a more detailed exploration of some of the planning issues raised by these examples.

Differentiation

Differentiation is one important aspect of short term planning, whether formal or informal – indeed, many commentators argue that differentiation is the key to ensuring access to the curriculum for pupils with special educational needs (Carpenter, 1992). Any or all of the levels of planning we have discussed in this book so far will benefit from being well–differentiated. As we have seen, Dearing's review brings the theoretical ideal of a differentiated National Curriculum within the grasp of all pupils. Working at the earliest levels of achievement within Key Stage 3 can now be a practical reality (see section 1).

We have also explored the notion of units of work, differentiated in terms of sequence and progression for particular age groups of pupils (see sections 4 and 5). We now wish to examine differentiation at the level of lesson, task, activity or session planning – at the interface between the proposed curriculum and the learning needs of individual pupils. Ann Lewis (1992) offers a thorough analysis of a range of possible varieties of differentiation and the following material borrows heavily from her ideas. Lewis proposes that adjusting tasks to the various interests, needs, aptitudes, experiences and previous achievements of diverse groups of pupils may entail thinking about:

- **content** – so that pupils work on various aspects of the same subject matter, for example, a reading activity focusing upon social sight recognition for some pupils and phonic word attack skills for others.

- **interest** – ensuring that activities have relevance to pupils' own experience and sources of motivation.

- **level** – enabling pupils to work on similar concepts at levels which reflect their previous achievements, so that, in the course of a lesson about plants as living things, one pupil may confirm the idea that plants need water in order to live while a second pupil comes to understand that the roots of a plant draw moisture up out of the soil.

- **access** – so that material is presented to pupils through various modes, whether aural, visual, tactile, concrete, symbolic, linguistic or via information technology.

- **structure** – whereby work may be presented, for instance, in small, developmentally sequenced, subject specific steps for some pupils and in conceptually holistic, integrated chunks for others.

60

- **sequence** – allowing pupils access to material in varying orders which may be planned in advance or determined spontaneously by pupil preference.

- **pace** – encouraging pupils to work through material at varying speeds, again, either because work is presented to them at different rates or because they are encouraged to determine their own preferred pace.

- **response** – acknowledging that pupils will respond to similar activities in varied ways, either because the teacher has planned to request different outcomes from different individual pupils or because pupils spontaneously respond in different ways.

- **staff time** – allowing individual pupils different amounts and qualities of staff support, varying from intensive 1:1 input, through pauses permitting delayed responses, to occasional guidance for pupils working essentially independently.

- **teaching style** – ensuring that pupils experience a range of approaches to teaching from didactic classroom presentations, through investigative, experiential fieldwork, to discursive tutorials.

- **learning style** – giving pupils opportunities to respond to teaching in a variety of ways, whether by listening passively , participating actively in explorations and discoveries, or taking the lead in solving problems.

- **grouping** – offering a balance of individual, paired, group, class, departmental and whole school learning experiences.

It is worth noting here that these forms of differentiation can be distinguished broadly in terms of differentiated input and outcome. Further, many of these strategies can encourage both detailed teacher planning and pupil self differentiation. Clearly, effective planning for differentiation depends upon accurate assessment of pupils' prior achievements; considered diagnosis of future learning needs, and tightly focused target setting. This may itself be a process which is negotiated between teacher and pupil. At other times, however, staff will wish to allow pupils to self-differentiate, particularly where tasks are open-ended or investigative, encouraging pupils to develop their own access strategies to shared activities and to pursue varied outcomes. Staff in these instances should be prepared to observe pupils' approaches to problem solving and exploration and to record the resulting differentiated responses.

There is no suggestion here that all of these aspects of differentiation should be called into play in every lesson. This is not a checklist of imperatives but a suggested range of possibilities. Staff will need to decide when to control differentiation and when to facilitate pupil-directed learning. Different sessions and subjects will lend themselves to various forms of differentiation according to the curricular aims which apply and the group of pupils involved. Individual teachers or teachers working in teams may wish to work through some of these ideas, however, as an aid to planning particular sessions or sequences of sessions. Subject co-ordinators may introduce the notion of a differentiation audit (Galloway and Banes, 1994) to colleagues as part of their responsibility for monitoring curriculum implementation (see section 8). This set of ideas will then constitute a useful prompt for focused discussion and an agenda for development. Figure 6:4 offers a blank format which staff may wish to photocopy for note taking in these discussions.

Group work

We have noted the use of group work as one aspect of differentiating learning opportunities. Many activities proposed by the National Curriculum actively require pupils to work together in groups (Byers, 1994b) and the *Guidance* on the inspection schedule (Ofsted, 1995) makes it clear that learning to work in a range of groupings is an important part of education for all pupils, whether judgements are being made about standards of achievement, quality of learning or quality of teaching. The debate about group work has been pursued in detail elsewhere (McCall, 1983; Rose, 1991; Sebba, Byers and Rose, 1993). Suffice it to say here that teachers will wish to consider the purpose and constitution of groups in their planning. For example, groups may be:

● homogeneous – a set of pupils whose learning needs are broadly alike and who are expected to be able to work together on a shared task at a comparable rate and towards similar outcomes;
● heterogeneous – a mixed grouping of pupils who bring significantly varied prior experiences, achievements and aptitudes to a shared task.

Many schools, faced with the challenge of classes of pupils of widely differing abilities, choose to adopt a strategy whereby pupils with similar needs are grouped together. In some instances, pupils are withdrawn from class in small groups to work together in a geographical location which is separate from their peers. The rationale for this strategy is that pupils of like ability work together effectively and that those pupils with the most complex needs do not impede the progress of the rest of the class. There may, indeed, be a justification for creating homogeneous sets of pupils, both those experiencing difficulties in achieving and those whose rapid prior progress indicates the need for enrichment activity, on occasion. These sorts of temporary groupings for specific activities should not be confused with permanent forms of segregation. Streamed groupings deny the benefits which a well-differentiated approach may offer to all pupils and fail to recognise that pupils require opportunities to play a variety of roles in learning situations. The line between differentiation and discrimination can, at times, become somewhat thin (Hart, 1992) and teachers need to consider with great care their reasons for grouping pupils. Research in the area of collaborative learning does, in fact, suggest that all pupils, both the high achievers and those experiencing difficulties, make the greatest progress, both academically and socially, when working in fully integrated groups (Swing and Peterson, 1982; Johnson and Johnson, 1983; Slavin, 1988).

Jigsawing

It may be possible to focus the differentiation more tightly within groups by allocating information, materials, resources and responsibilities to particular pupils, or, indeed, by inviting the pupils to make their own decisions about their individual roles in the group. This technique has been referred to as jigsawing (Rose, 1991) and may be used to:

● promote the development of new skills, concepts, knowledge and understanding;
● encourage the maintenance, consolidation, demonstration in new contexts and generalisation of existing skills, concepts, knowledge and understanding.

Jigsawing has been used most successfully as a means of addressing the individual needs of pupils in group teaching situations. It has been particularly helpful to those teachers planning activities to include pupils with a wide range of special needs.

In jigsawing, the individual components of an activity are identified, and the needs of pupils matched to these components. The emphasis upon planning has two main thrusts:

- to encourage pupils to work collaboratively, and develop their skills of interaction and sociability;
- to ensure that all pupils participate at an appropriate level, and that their individual needs are addressed.

This approach can be best illustrated through an example of its use which in this case was produced by teachers on a SENSE curriculum management course in Bradford. Figure 6:5 lists a class of Key Stage 2 pupils who attend a school for pupils with severe learning difficulties. These pupils have a wide range of needs and abilities, including profound and multiple learning difficulties, sensory impairments, and autistic traits. Such a mix of pupils has become increasingly common in some special schools in recent years. The class has been asked, as part of a technology lesson, to make a guy for the coming school bonfire night celebrations.

Pupil's individual priorities to be addressed during technology lessons have been identified. In some instances these can be seen to have a social emphasis, whilst in others the priorities are more closely related to an academic curriculum.

The requirement for this group is to plan the activity to encourage collaborative learning, whilst addressing some of the established individual priorities.

Figure 6:6 is the chart used to plan the activity. In column one, the making of a guy has been divided into three parts. These parts consist of a series of activities which, when combined, will result in the production of the guy. Group one involves three pupils in choosing clothes, and stuffing these with paper to make the guy's body. Group two is concerned with joining the parts of the guy together, and group three with producing a mask for the guy. The activity in itself is nothing unusual, and given the task to produce a guy, it is likely that most teachers would adopt a similar approach.

In column two, consideration has been given to the way in which pupils will be matched to the three activities. Recognition is given to the individual priorities set for pupils, along with physical needs, and the level of support required. It can, for instance, be seen that Mike's improving motor skills are being addressed through encouraging the use of scissors, Susan's numeracy requirements have been considered, and related to her part of the activity, and an opportunity has been created to address Neil's physical needs.

In order to be a group activity, rather than a collection of individual tasks, opportunities for collaboration need to be addressed. In the second group, Susan and Paul are being encouraged to assist each other by holding the material taut whilst their partner sews. In the third group, a collective decision between Mike and Judy is required before Judy completes her part of the task. The three groups are interdependent. The activity cannot succeed unless each group completes its part of the process. This means that opportunities exist for pupils to share their work, and for the teacher to encourage communication and co-operation between the groups.

Teachers using the jigsawing approach need to be aware of the 'Blue Peter' factor. Because the groups are dependent upon each other, and not all will work at the same pace, it is necessary to prepare some of the work beforehand in order that pupils are not waiting too long for the earlier parts of the process to be completed. In the example given here, group two require some sewing work before group one have finished their part of the task.

Column three recognises that opportunities exist to assess the progress which some pupils are making in relation to their individual priorities. It also acknowledges that it is not practical to expect that every pupil's progress will be assessed during a lesson, and that it is more realistic to concentrate only upon two or three pupils.

Planning for group activity in this way is a relatively simple process. When used consistently, it has the advantage of identifying before the lesson those parts of an activity which will be most readily addressed by individual pupils. It also enables the teacher to ensure that individual priorities having been established are considered during each lesson.

It is not suggested that all pupils in the example given, or in any other jigsawed activity, will participate for the whole session. It is recognised that different pupils have varying attention spans, and in some instances physical needs will restrict the length of participation. Planning in this way does ensure that the opportunities to make best use of limited participation, by matching needs to the activity, can be taken. In the example given, Alan's priority of remaining on task for five minutes can be addressed in the activity matched to his need. He is making a contribution to the lesson by identifying clothes to be used for the guy, but his withdrawal if necessary after five minutes will not totally disrupt the group.

Jigsawed activities do not have to be broken down into three groups. Some activities lend themselves more easily to four groups or in some cases just two. Much will depend upon what is most easily managed in the class situation, and the number of staff available to assist with the approach.

Figure 6:7 provides a blank chart for planning jigsawed activities and for identifying individual pupil priorities.

Clearly, jigsawed activity may be planned to encourage a mix of new endeavour and familiar activity. It is worth noting, however, that learning to collaborate may itself constitute a fresh challenge for many pupils, suggesting that this may be a good time to rehearse established skills, and that groups working on new areas of learning may require increased staff support.

Envoying

Amongst other group work approaches which have proved useful for involving pupils with special needs, 'envoying' is one which can be of particular use when addressing communication difficulties. This has been successfully deployed in a number of primary schools, and in particular those which use a thematic approach.

In envoying a pupil is used as a carrier of information (envoy) between groups of pupils working on different aspects of a related theme. For example, in a class where pupils are working on the production of a brochure to advertise the Great Exhibition of 1851 as part of a Victorian history study unit, one group may be investigating the latest inventions and industrial developments of this period, whilst another is considering the layout and format of the brochure. An envoy, or series of envoys, will be used to carry information from one group to the other, to assist each other in the overall planning of the brochure (see Figures 6:8 and 6:9).

The roles of the envoy are made clear in Figure 6:10. For a pupil with communication difficulties this may prove to be a daunting task. Support can be provided (6.10) by pairing a pupil for the role of envoy. In the example given here, Nigel is expected to report on only one piece of information. He is encouraged to use both written and pictorial information for support, and has been provided with an opportunity to rehearse his role with Rachel. The role played by Rachel needs to be carefully defined. She should be there as a support, and not to take over the responsibilities given to Nigel. She should also be able to prompt him should he have difficulties in providing information. As Nigel gains in confidence in this role, the amount of information which he carries can be increased, and the support provided by one of his peers gradually diminished.

For some pupils, the task of communication may be supported by use of information technology, such as a Liberator or Orac communicator, or through a communication board, or the use of a symbol system. Confidence in communication, and an understanding of the importance of interaction with a group, will only be achieved if pupils with special needs are given an equal opportunity to participate fully in this role.

Whichever approach to promoting group work and interaction is developed in schools, teachers must be aware that for all pupils, the skills necessary to participate as part of a group need to be learned. Both envoying and jigsawing have a proven worth in promoting group work, but both take time to establish, and success in their use will seldom be achieved immediately. A key role for teachers should be in the promotion of social interaction amongst pupils; this will not be achieved through the perpetual use of individual teaching sessions, and the importance of developing effective group work strategies is essential if this goal is to be attained.

Staff interested in sharing views about group work may like to contact the Collaborative Learning Project at 17, Barford Street, London, N1 0QB.

Planning for individual pupils

Short term planning for individual pupils should be an integral part of the individual education planning and annual review processes described in the *Code of Practice* (DfE, 1994). It may take account of both subject related targets (such as demonstrating an ability to use historical sources to draw conclusions or recognising some of the different ways in which musical sounds are made) and cross-curricular aspects of the curriculum. Many schools are finding that progression, continuity and relevance are enhanced for individual pupils when learning targets are set in terms of cross-curricular skills and pursued in the context of subject related activity. This constitutes a truly integrated approach (Byers, 1992) whereby pupils are offered access to activity founded in the programmes of study for the subjects of the National Curriculum and, at the same time, make progress towards highly individualised targets devised in response to honest perceptions of priority need (see sections 2 and 4).

Figures 6:11 and 6:12 show two responses to the task of planning individual targets which will be addressed across the curriculum. In Figure 6:11, targets identified at Annual Review are entered on the pupil's Individual Learning Focus sheet, using categories of cross-curricular skills. ILF Tracking blanks are then made available to subject teachers for the recording of responses in a range of contexts across the curriculum. In Figure 6:11 we see notes made in relation to food technology sessions.

Figure 6:12 shows the targets set by a special educational needs co-ordinator for a pupil spending increasing amounts of time included in classes beyond his special unit. She establishes both subject specific targets, based on the records which have come back to her from subject teachers in previous terms, and cross-curricular PSE targets, which she feels will promote consistency of intent and approach from staff throughout the teaching week. These individual targets will contribute to the planning of well-differentiated activity in subject specific lessons while the records of responses which staff will make in relation to these targets will drive the setting of revised targets and, ultimately, reporting and Annual Review (see section 7).

Figure 6:13 offers a blank format bringing together many of these principles. It allows staff, and pupil, to note both cross-curricular and subject-related targets. It gives space for a record of experience over a series of sessions – information which may be duplicated for groups of pupils. It permits the noting of significant learning outcomes, dated and, where schools prefer, coded, as a record of achievement. The lower sections encourage staff and pupils to discuss new targets at the end of a unit of work; give space for an evaluation of the activities themselves; and facilitate formal assessment of progress made. This may be referenced back to the assessment opportunities which were built into schemes of work at the planning stage (see section 5) and may be moderated in discussion with subject co-ordinators, providing useful information for curriculum review (see section 8).

Breadth and balance

Individual target setting may mean that balance in the curriculum appears idiosyncratic for a particular pupil at any given time. Staff, in consultation with the pupil, the parents and often other professionals, (DfE, 1994) may deliberately create short term imbalance in order to address specific issues of relevance and priority. For instance:

- a pupil with English as a second home language may benefit from a finite period of immersion in language activity;
- a pupil recovering from corrective surgery may require an intensive programme of frequent, regular physiotherapy;
- a recently bereaved pupil may need to spend time experiencing the support of a counselling relationship in place of regular lessons.

Each of these examples of temporary curricular enrichment is consistent with the definition of the whole curriculum which we explored in section 2. The task for staff is to ensure that pupils receive an entitlement to breadth over time even where balance is variable in the short term.

In the same way, learning priorities for pupils with particular needs may dictate an emphasis on certain areas of the curriculum in the longer term. For example:

- achieving an appropriate position prior to engaging in curriculum-related activity is likely to demand significant amounts of time, and staff support, for a pupil with cerebral palsy;
- time devoted to multi-sensory, tactile and olfactory experiences is likely to be of long term benefit to a pupil who is isolated from peers, from staff and from the visual and aural environment by sensory impairments;
- regular individual sessions of music therapy may help to maintain a pupil with social and communicative difficulties in integrated class groupings for most of the time.

Again, these variations in conventional balance are encompassed by the whole curriculum definition offered by National Curriculum Council (1990); elaborated for pupils with severe learning difficulties in Curriculum Guidance 9 (NCC, 1992) and taken forward for all pupils by SCAA (1995).

Progression and continuity

Records of experience based on curriculum planning documentation may be used to audit the breadth of the curriculum offered to pupils over time (see section 7). Responses to individual learning needs may dictate variations in balance in the short, medium or long term but individual target setting will ensure both progression through a pupil's school experiences over time and continuity of intent and approach across the curriculum. Individual targets thus lend coherence to learning opportunities which may otherwise become fragmented and inconsistent.

Lesson plan			
Subject: Science	**Date:** 2.5.95	**Week:** 9	**Class:** JS

What do you want the pupils to learn?

Group 1 & 2:   that some items conduct electricity
Group 3:   work on making circuits to work buzzer or switch

What the pupils are actually going to do:

Group 1 & 2: experiment and test different items to see if they conduct electricity or not; put into sets; observe properties of items in sets

Group 3: further work on simple circuits; use bulb, switch, buzzer; answer questions as they work

Resource needs:

Electricity resource box

Any necessary classroom organisational issues:

Group 1: MB, FP;   Group 2: HG, LM, BC;   Group 3: JH, WD, KT
Groups 1 & 2 work with CA and college student
Group 3 work individually, supervision from JS and work experience student

Learning outcomes:

Group 1: FP realised that 'metal' conducts, predicted 'make it work' each time, carried out own checks on circuit connections when testing

Group 2: LM absent. BC very experimental, eventually realised that 'metal' objects 'worked', needs more experience

Group 3 need more work on circuits: KT still unsure; JH competent most of time & enjoyed experimenting; WD had fine motor problems but said and gestured wires to connect

Figure 6.1 From Dycorts School

Scheme of Work

Subject: PE: games **Date:** Summer 95 **Day:** Monday **Time:** 2 to 2.45

Group: Junior 2   **Staff:** Mary, Jenny, Sue

Group A: Nicky, Josh, Vivec, Liam, Maria, Gemma
Group B: Simon, Helen, Bobby, Andrea

Aims:

Encourage physical activity and positive participation through enjoyment

Learning objectives:

Pupils should be taught to:
develop basic ball skills, throwing & receiving etc.
use equipment in a variety of ways
co-operate in pairs and groups
develop safe practices

Assessment opportunities:

National Curriculum PE, Key Stage 1: develop and practise a variety of ways
of sending, receiving and travelling with a ball
School physical curriculum, level 1

Activities:

Group A: partner work: bouncing, rolling, throwing, aiming, catching
small group work: games to develop spatial awareness, passing
skills, (see activity bank) nb two-handed straight pass in running
games, co-operation, playing to simple rules

Group B: focus on equipment, experiment, play
work in pairs on grasp, release, hold, pull
group game: rolling ball to named target
Helen and Bobby: physiotherapy work in addition to group targets

Resources:

Games equipment in hall

Recording:

Skills sheets to be updated each
session. Complete Activity Recording
Sheets at end of half term for files.

Evaluation:

Group A: more work on individual skills needed prior to games
Group B: try rolling to sound targets as well as visual;
use variety of sizes, textures, colours etc. of balls

Figure 6.2 From Montacute School

Activities planning sheet		

Date: Jan to Feb 95   **Key Stage:** 3   **Class:** 9B

Title: Roman Empire (History)

Week:	Plan:	Reality:
1	Quick revision of timeline Map of Roman Empire; Zig Zag 1	Revision of timeline Map of Roman Empire; Latin names Extracts from Zig Zag 1
2	Pompeii; Zig Zag 3 Roman economy	Zig Zag 3; how do we know about Pompeii? matching Roman & modern objects; sorting coins
3	Being an archaeologist handling session prepare for museum visit	practise handling artefacts observation & discussion watch Time Teams
4	Bedford Museum blanket dig observe & record artefacts	Blanket dig at Bedford museum handling Roman objects question curator
5	Plaster casting Guiseppe Fiorelli	Recall museum trip observation, drawing use of recording sheets
6	Revision and assessment	Assessment Now and Then video

Key concepts:	Resources:
place events, people and changes within a chronological framework (KS3) investigate independently using artefacts, pictures, photos and film, buildings and sites (KS3) government, state, empire, republic, peasantry, trade, dictatorship (KS3)	Zig Zag video Time teams video Bedford museum Library Project collection Roman resource file

Figure 6.3 From Grange School

70

Planning for differentiation

Session focus:

content	response
interest	structure
pace	teacher time
sequence	teaching style
level	learning style
access	grouping

Figure 6.4

71

Characteristics of Pupils in the Group and Priorities for Technology Sessions

Sanjay has cerebral palsy. Limited movement of limbs. Left hand slightly easier than right. Poor distance vision.

Individual priorities. Co-operation with an adult in practical activities.

Susan has good levels of verbal communication, but poor concentration. Behaviour can be difficult when challenged or if she does not wish to co-operate.

Individual priorities. Sharing materials with other pupils. Counting to ten.

Jenny. Proficient Makaton user. Likes to please. Easily distracted, and rarely settles to an activity for more than a few minutes.

Individual priorities. Improved pencil control. Increased attention to task.

Neil. Profound and multiple learning difficulties. Very sociable. Very stiff arms, but developing grasp.

Individual priorities. Extending arms to reach for objects. Maintaining visual attention to objects placed in front of him.

Paul. Autistic tendencies. Level of co-operation variable. Enjoys mechanical/repetitive activities. Unpredictable behaviour. Good understanding of language, but no speech.

Individual priorities. To remain in the room throughout a twenty minute activity. To complete a fine motor task lasting five minutes.

Mike. Developing Makaton user. Good concentration. Improving motor skills, eager to please, but easily frustrated if success does not come quickly.

Individual priorities. To improve control in tool use – pencil, scissors, brushes. To increase Makaton vocabulary related to technology lessons, and to improve consistency in signing.

Judy. Withdrawn pupil who likes to work alone. Does not like adult intervention. A few spoken words. Good language comprehension but very stubborn.

Individual priorities. To change activities without losing temper. To participate as part of a group. To use please and thankyou consistently.

Alan. No speech. Very passive and difficult to motivate. Good visual skills. Enjoys company of peers, but not often willing to co-operate in group activities.

Individual priorities. To share materials with peers. To remain on task for five minutes. To complete a visual activity alone.

Figure 6.5

JIGSAWED GROUP ACTIVITY – Making a Guy for Bonfire Night

ACTIVITY	PUPILS	ASSESSMENT FOCUS
Pupils choosing clothes for the guy. Tying ends of arms and legs of clothes. Stuffing clothing with paper.	Alan to match clothes to pictures Neil and Sanjay to be helped to screw up newspaper and stuff it into clothing	Neil's ability to reach for paper, and take paper from an adult.
Pupils using large sewing needles with string to join parts of the guy.	Susan and Paul to complete sewing. Paul to thread needles. Each pupil to hold material in place whilst the other sews.	Susan's ability to count (stitches) to ten, and to indicate more and less (number of stitches).
Pupils designing a mask for the guy. Choosing materials and making the mask.	Jenny to draw design. Mike to cut out materials and to give these to Judy. With Judy to decide where they should go on the mask. Judy to stick materials to mask	Mike's use of scissors to cut along a straight line drawn on stiff material (using large scissors).

Figure 6.6

JIGSAWED GROUP ACTIVITY

ACTIVITY	PUPILS	ASSESSMENT FOCUS

Figure 6.7

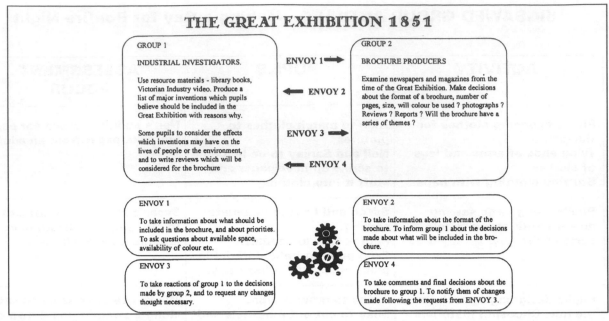

THE GREAT EXHIBITION 1851

GROUP 1

INDUSTRIAL INVESTIGATORS.

Use resource materials - library books, Victorian Industry video. Produce a list of major inventions which pupils believe should be included in the Great Exhibition with reasons why.

Some pupils to consider the effects which inventions may have on the lives of people or the environment, and to write reviews which will be considered for the brochure

ENVOY 1 →
← ENVOY 2
ENVOY 3 →
← ENVOY 4

GROUP 2

BROCHURE PRODUCERS

Examine newspapers and magazines from the time of the Great Exhibition. Make decisions about the format of a brochure, number of pages, size, will colour be used ? photographs ? Reviews ? Reports ? Will the brochure have a series of themes ?

ENVOY 1

To take information about what should be included in the brochure, and about priorities. To ask questions about available space, availability of colour etc.

ENVOY 3

To take reactions of group 1 to the decisions made by group 2, and to request any changes thought necessary.

ENVOY 2

To take information about the format of the brochure. To inform group 1 about the decisions made about what will be included in the brochure.

ENVOY 4

To take comments and final decisions about the brochure to group 1. To notify them of changes made following the requests from ENVOY 3.

Figure 6.8

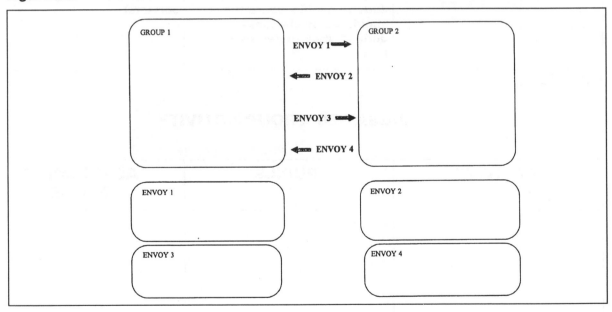

GROUP 1

ENVOY 1 →
← ENVOY 2
ENVOY 3 →
← ENVOY 4

GROUP 2

ENVOY 1

ENVOY 2

ENVOY 3

ENVOY 4

Figure 6.9

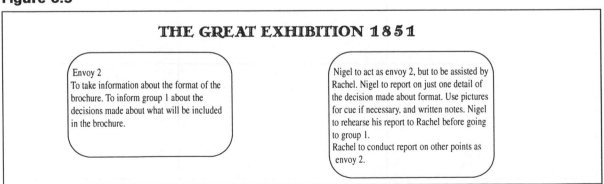

THE GREAT EXHIBITION 1851

Envoy 2
To take information about the format of the brochure. To inform group 1 about the decisions made about what will be included in the brochure.

Nigel to act as envoy 2, but to be assisted by Rachel. Nigel to report on just one detail of the decision made about format. Use pictures for cue if necessary, and written notes. Nigel to rehearse his report to Rachel before going to group 1.
Rachel to conduct report on other points as envoy 2.

Figure 6.10

		INDIVIDUAL LEARNING FOCUS
NAME	CLASS SY YEAR 1994–1995	INDIVIDUAL LEARNING FOCUS

PERSONAL & SOCIAL	PSE	1 • To take responsibility for his own belongings 2 • To resist touching items on display
COMMUNICATION	C	1 • To listen & respond to simple instructions 2 • To recognise signs for Gentlemen's Toilet, Coca Cola and Macdonalds
NUMERACY	N	1 • To recognise and select £1 2 • To show awareness of 1 to 1 correspondence by relating counting to objects
PHYSICAL	P	1 • To carry object with both hands 2 • To reach out for objects using left arm 3 • To maintain level of mobility and stamina
PROBLEM SOLVING	PS	1 • To locate requested members of staff 2 • To find his way around the Student Years department, locate the Office, Hall and Studio in the main school
INFORMATION TECHNOLOGY	IT	1 • To use Touch Screen and/or Concept Keyboard to activate auditory/visual response of his choice
STUDY SKILLS	SS	1 • To co-operate with his peers in a group situation

		I•L•F TRACKING
NAME	CLASS SY YEAR 1994–1995	I•L•F TRACKING SUBJECT EVIDENCE F. TEC

PERSONAL & SOCIAL	PSE	① Took shopping list & purse on trip to shops
COMMUNICATION	C	① Put on his apron and washed his hands ② Went to correct toilet when asked to wash his hands
NUMERACY	N	① Selected £1 to pay for his shopping ② Got out 3 plates
PHYSICAL	P	① Carried tray from breakfast bar to table ③ Walked to supermarket and back without help
PROBLEM SOLVING	PS	① Asked Irene to tie his apron, as requested
INFORMATION TECHNOLOGY	IT	① Used concept keyboard and food overlay to select his choice of money
STUDY SKILLS	SS	① Waited to use the can opener as Jonathan was using it.

Figure 6.11 From Woodlands School

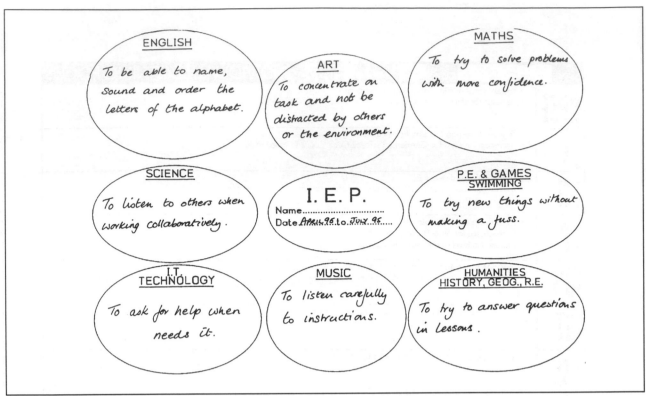

Figure 6.12a

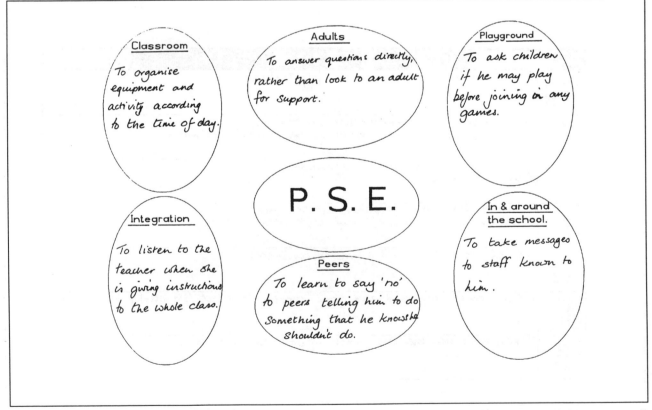

Figure 6.12b From Grange School

Class:	Name:	Curriculum Area:	Unit title:	Term:
subject specific **targets** cross-curricular **priorities**	sequence of **activity** record of **experience**	significant new **responses** record of **achievement**	**dates** **codes**	
proposed new **targets/priorities**	activity **review and evaluation**	continuous **assessment**	**agreed by:**	

Figure 6.13

SECTION 7

Issues in assessment, recording and reporting

The processes involved in assessment, recording and reporting have received considerable attention in most schools. Yet they are still seen as an area of difficulty which schools struggle to develop in a format which is usable and manageable and which adequately meets the needs of all pupils and teachers. In some schools it is still possible to find a wide range of approaches being used and, whilst many of these may be effective in their own right, a lack of consistency across a school has a detrimental effect upon planning and curriculum delivery. Chesworth (1994) demonstrated the value of in-school collaboration in the development of a co-ordinated response to record keeping. As she rightly states, the relationship between assessment, recording and reporting and all other aspects of the curriculum is a complex one and, for this reason, concentration upon any of these in isolation from the whole process of curriculum development is likely to lead to difficulties and frustrations. In this book, we have endeavoured to illustrate, through examples, opportunities which exist for incorporating assessment, recording and reporting at all stages of the curriculum development process. In this section we will consider some of the relationships between these important elements and other aspects of the curriculum.

Recognising opportunities at the planning stage

The *Code of Practice* (DfE, 1994) emphasises the importance of involving pupils at all stages of the education process. This includes planning, recording, assessment and reporting.

Schools should consider how they:

- involve pupils in decision making processes;
- determine the pupil's level of participation, taking into account approaches to assessment and intervention which are suitable for his or her age, ability and past experiences;
- record pupil's views in identifying their difficulties, setting goals, agreeing a development strategy, monitoring and reviewing progress;
- involve pupils in implementing individual education plans. (para. 2.37).

Recent research suggests that few schools have made significant progress in meeting these requirements in all areas (MacNamara and Rose, 1995). Whilst some have made moves towards pupil involvement in evaluation of their own learning, the number of schools involving them at the planning stage is still relatively small. Hardwick and Rushton (1994) describe the potential which exists for greater involvement of pupils with special needs in action planning, a process which they see as critical in developing pupil's skills of communication, negotiation, and understanding of intended learning outcomes. Galton (1989) also emphasises the importance of the pupil/teacher dialogue, during which agreed standards for performance can be reached and mutual criteria for assessment established. Pupils involved at the planning stage (see section 6) have a clearer view of teacher expectations; can be assisted in identifying areas of work which may cause them difficulties; and have an opportunity to feel valued in the whole learning process.

The involvement of pupils at the planning stage can be seen as a means of establishing learning targets and discussing how these will be achieved. Equally valuable may be the opportunity to link learning to other aspects of the pupil's development. In some instances teachers have divorced social and emotional development from other aspects of pupil's learning. For example, programmes have been written with the intention of changing behaviour and have focused upon those details of behaviour which present a challenge without linking these to teaching intentions and learning outcomes. As Charlton and David (1989) stated:

> Although learning difficulties may be present without behaviour problems, and behaviour problems may be shown separately, they often coexist. (page 70)

Figures 7:1 and 7:2 provide an example of how planning by a teacher, directly involving a pupil with emotional and behavioural difficulties, links learning outcomes to behaviour. In this example, the teacher has negotiated a learning target in mathematics with the pupil which will be assessed by both the teacher and the pupil. A similar process has been undertaken to identify a behaviour target for the maths lessons, also to be assessed by both parties. Both learning and behaviour have been given an overall target score, again agreed between teacher and pupil. At the end of the week's maths lesson, learning and behaviour is assessed by both teacher and pupil and their assessment moderated by a pupil, chosen by the pupil being assessed, and by another member of staff, in this example a classroom assistant who has worked with the pupil.

In the example given, the approach developed aimed to increase the pupil's self esteem by giving them some responsibility for their own learning and behaviour. The format serves not only to involve the pupil in planning, but also in self assessment, evaluation and reporting. Amongst other advantages of this approach is the fact that it encourages dialogue between the pupil and the teacher which is focused upon both learning and behaviour. An opportunity is created for the sharing of views, during which the teacher can make known his intentions for the pupil, whilst the pupil can express anxieties and the stresses which are related to both learning and social and emotional needs.

Clarity of intention is an important feature of good teaching. The pupil who has an understanding of teacher expectations, and has shared in the planning process, feels valued and has an increased incentive to perform well. Action planning and the sharing of objectives require a positive relationship between the teacher and the pupil. A partnership based upon trust and respect must be established but this process can, in itself, be an important element in influencing the development of a positive attitude to learning. Establishing this approach need not be a complicated procedure, but the provision of some form of agreement between teacher and pupil is necessary if it is to operate smoothly.

Figures 7:3 and 7:4 provide a simple example of how teacher planning and student/pupil input can be combined. On these sheets, the pupil has an opportunity to comment upon her priorities within a subject, whilst the teacher must still declare his objectives for the pupil. In addition to the statement about planning, the same sheets contain an area for reporting upon progress. This is followed by a box to be used for an agreed statement which can be signed by both the teacher and the student.

Such approaches are being developed in many schools, including those for pupils with severe learning difficulties (Lawson, 1992; Hardwick and Rushton, 1994). Symbol systems, or other forms of augmented communication, have been used to good effect in enabling pupils with learning or communication difficulties to gain access to action planning. Fergusson (1994) has indicated the importance of seeing such approaches as part of a continuum which, whilst providing an end in themselves for some pupils, will be seen as a step towards more complex forms of communication for many. Pupils who do not use traditional orthography should not be denied access to joint planning and, indeed, many teachers who have become proficient in the use of photographs and video recording for recording progress and experience are now beginning to explore the same media as an aid to pupil involvement in planning. This, at the simplest level, may begin with the use of symbols, pictures or photographs on personal timetables and may be followed by lesson planning sheets which include lesson content and intended outcomes.

The planning stage is critical for the effective monitoring of learning outcomes (see section 5). Plans should, of course, relate directly to school policy, to schemes of work, and to individual education programmes (see relevant sections in this book). The planning stage may equally serve as a guideline during the curriculum monitoring process when the subject co-ordinator is attempting to make observations concerning breadth and balance (see section 8).

Assessment

Throughout this book we have emphasised the place of assessment as an integral part of the teaching process, built into the curriculum and not added on at a later stage. Assessment is largely about the collection of evidence related to what has been taught and what pupils have learned. As such it should inform teachers and enable them to plan more effectively. Assessment is not synonymous with testing and, whilst tests may have a place in the assessment of pupils, they should not be used exclusively to make decisions about pupil progress. Assessment should relate directly to pupil needs and to teaching. Rouse (1991) has described the way in which testing has become almost ritualistic in some schools and education authorities, conducted on a regular basis to provide statistics which have little direct bearing upon what happens in the classroom. The introduction of politically motivated educational 'league tables', which supply charts of figures and encourage generalised statements about the performances of schools, have little intrinsic value in a system which aims to support teachers in addressing the needs of a diverse population. Of far greater value to schools, and to the pupils within them, is a system which values assessment as a means of identifying the progress which pupils make and assists in the planning of a route for further development. Sir Ron Dearing (1993a,

1993b), in recognising the value of teacher assessment and the integrity of the profession in monitoring the learning of all pupils, has made significant moves towards placing an emphasis upon classroom based assessment procedures as opposed to standardised tests.

Assessment in schools can be seen to have two main functions.

◆ Summative – whereby an assessment is made, following a course of teaching, to see what learning has taken place and what has been retained by a pupil or group of pupils. Summative assessment can also used to ascertain the effectiveness of teaching methods, resources and groupings.

◆ Formative – whereby the information gained through assessment is used to inform planning and to address continuity of learning.

Assessment for its own sake is of little value. Assessment should only be undertaken if the information gained is to be used. This will generally be as an indication of progress, or as a means of identifying areas for future development.

Figures 7:5 and 7:6 provide one format for combining both summative and formative assessment to assist with planning for continuity.

In this example, there is a planning element which describes what will be taught in an English course during the term. At the end of the term, these plans are re-examined in relation to more explicit detail of the course content. This section may be of some help to a subject co-ordinator (see section 8) who needs to ensure appropriate coverage of the subject and could be used as part of an ongoing record. The actual participation of a pupil with special needs is recorded in relation to the term's subject coverage. More importantly, it can be seen that the teacher has identified opportunities to address objectives set for the pupil through the annual review and comments on how these were used during the term. The section on forward planning is used to indicate how, in the coming term, the teacher will continue to address the individual needs of the pupil and will build upon the work of the current term.

This approach could, of course, be used in conjunction with the principles described earlier of negotiation with the pupil to ensure a common understanding of what is to be achieved. Equally, involving the pupil in self evaluation related to the objectives set may play an important role in developing pupil confidence and ensuring clarity of purpose.

A great deal has been written about pupil self evaluation in recent years (Lawson, 1992; NCC, 1992; Hardwick and Rushton, 1994), and many schools have begun to involve pupils in expressing their opinions related to the lessons they receive and their own performance. *Curriculum Guidance 9* (NCC, 1992) provided examples of ways in which pupils could contribute to the assessment process, ranging from simple statements about 'things I can do by myself', to the more sophisticated use of information technology to indicate how well a pupil feels she performs in a specific curriculum area. Consultation with pupils about their experiences and achievements has been recognised as an important process in many schools for a number of years. Pupils make valuable comments on their own progress and on their aspirations for future learning through end of year reports and often by attending parent consultation evenings. Pupils with special needs have equally valid contributions to make in this area and, with careful consideration of the media to be used to provide access, this can generally be achieved.

Schools have developed a range of self evaluation approaches and have used a variety of media, including photographs, video, tape recordings and the collection of drawings and other work, to contribute to records of achievement. In developing such a variety of approaches, schools need to establish some consistency in order to ensure that pupils know what is expected of them. Teachers also need to build in criteria which are clearly understood by pupils, in order that statements which they make may be objective and genuinely reflect learning. Statements such as 'I can' need to be qualified by evidence, much of which can be collated by the teacher, but which should be supported by the confidence of the pupil who knows that an accurate assessment has been made.

Figure 7:7 takes the role of the pupil in self evaluation beyond the simple 'I can' statement by including two further elements. Firstly the 'I can' statement is qualified by clear criteria – 'I know I can do this because . . .' Secondly, evidence is to be compiled which further supports the assessment. The pupil knows that she can complete the task described (in this case naming and sorting shapes), because she has recognised that an assessment was made of the task on two separate dates. In addition to this the teacher has accumulated evidence to support the assessment and has discussed this with the pupil.

Throughout this section we have argued that pupils should play a full part in assessment, recording and reporting procedures. We have given examples of how this may be achieved. This philosophy, further reflected in other sections of this book, builds upon the belief that education should be concerned with far more than the provision of skills and knowledge. It should develop independence and autonomy which cannot be achieved unless teachers enter into a partnership with their pupils (Tilstone, 1991) and encourage them to take some responsibility for their own learning.

NAME Michael Jones   SUBJECT Maths   WEEK BEGINNING 16.1.95

AGREED TARGET SCORE = 26   MODERATED BY (STAFF) K. Mann   (STUDENT) Ann Green

LEARNING TARGET	To input data from school grounds survey into data base "grass". To complete graph work begun last week, and to enter this neatly into the project file.	
TEACHER ASSESSMENT	Michael understands how to use the data base, but needs to be more accurate in entering data. Last week's work completed, but work entered in to file is rather untidy, with a number of errors, and needs attention.	7
		10
STUDENT ASSESSMENT	I enjoyed the computer work, but made a lot of mistakes with the numbers. Some of the graph work was boring, I needed more time for copying up neatly. Mr Pearce has agreed to let me tidy work up at home.	6
		10
PERSONAL TARGET	To work in a group with Joe without arguing. To walk away if Joe starts an argument. To begin work as soon as the lesson begins.	
TEACHER ASSESSMENT	Good sessions on Monday and Wednesday, let down by shouting at Joe on Thursday. Better prepared at the start of lessons, but still taking too long to settle down to work.	8
		10
STUDENT ASSESSMENT	I started the week well, but Joe still winds me up and I lose my temper. I find it hard to concentrate at the start of lessons because it is too noisy. I arrived at every maths lesson on time, and had everything I needed.	9
		10
AGREED STATEMENT	A much better week. Worked quite hard and enjoyed the computer work. Most work was completed well. Behaviour was mostly appropriate, and a lot of effort was made to stay on task. 2 bonus points awarded.	30
		40

Figure 7.1

NAME   SUBJECT   WEEK BEGINNING

AGREED TARGET SCORE =   MODERATED BY (STAFF)   (STUDENT)

LEARNING TARGET		
TEACHER ASSESSMENT		
		10
STUDENT ASSESSMENT		
		10
PERSONAL TARGET		
TEACHER ASSESSMENT		
		10
STUDENT ASSESSMENT		
		10
AGREED STATEMENT		
		40

Figure 7.2

TEACHER PLANNING AND RECORDING SHEET
(To be completed in conjunction with the student sheet)

STUDENTS NAME   SUBJECT   TERM

This term in   the course content will be:

       has identified the following areas for improvement:

He/she also needs to consider:

This term   did well in the following areas:

The following areas need more work during next term:

AGREED STATEMENT
This report has been shared with the student, and his/her report has also been shared.
The following statement has been agreed by both the student and teacher

---

Figure 7.3

STUDENT PLANNING AND RECORDING SHEET   NAME

SUBJECT   TERM

This term in   I will be doing:

The things I would like to do better at are:

The things which I enjoyed this term were:

The things which were not quite so good were:

I think I have improved at:

I still need to do better at:

Figure 7.4

Subject **English**	Term **Summer 1995**
Pupil **John Smith**	

What will be taught?

Poetry

First World War poets

Sassoon, Owen, Brooke.

Lord of the Flies

Writing

Eye witness accounts, writing journalist reports of an event during the term. Using journalist accounts from 1st World War, examining language and looking at metaphors.

What was covered?

Examination of emotions in the war poets. Pupils wrote poetry in the style of one of the poets.

Discussion of emotions and relationships carried on through work on *Lord of the Flies.* Some drama with pupils assuming roles based on the characters from the book.

Extracts from newspapers used to examine journalist styles. Accounts written by pupils of summer fayre, sports event and theatre trips.

What did he/she do?

John listened to tapes of the war poets, and answered questions on to tape. Demonstrated good understanding of vocabulary, and was able to put poetry into context of time. Not able to write a poem, but suggested ideas which were written by another pupil. Made good verbal contributions to discussion on *Lord of the Flies.* Made a 'radio broadcast' of school fayre which was used during lessons discussion on different reporting media. Listened well to archive recordings from war and commented on these.

Individual objectives from annual review.

To have the confidence to make greater verbal contributions in lessons.

To remain on task for periods of at least thirty minutes.

To use media other than written to express his ideas, and to be prepared to share his ideas with others in class.

To participate in practical activities in lessons, and to join in group activities.

Objectives addressed in the subject this term.

John did make good contributions to discussions on *Lord of the Flies,* a story which he enjoyed. This was provided for him on tape, and he clearly listened to all of it. Using tape recordings enabled John to work alone some of the time, but he was happy for these to be used in class, and this gave him more confidence to participate in class. We have encouraged John to use tape recordings, and in the journalism work this term tried to help him to see that radio broadcasts are a valuable source of information. This did encourage him to use his limited reading skills in developing cues for his recordings. John still reluctant to join in practical parts of the lesson, preferring to work alone.

Forward planning.

Next term we will be working on writing and producing a play. It will be difficult to encourage John to play a speaking role, and may be best to encourage him to contribute ideas for the writing in a workshop situation.

Figure 7.5

Subject	Term
Pupil	

What will be taught?	What was covered?	What did he/she do?

Individual objectives from annual review.

Objectives addressed in the subject this term.

Forward planning.

Figure 7.6

Mathematics Self Assessment

Pupil's name Amy Green

I can ...

Name and sort the shapes

square
circle
triangle

I know I can do it because ...

I did this without any help on 8th December 1994 and again on 4th February 1995. Mrs Wells made a video recording of me doing it.

(Dictated to Mrs Jones 4th Feb 1995)

Evidence collected
Work from Amy's maths book retained. Worksheets from school maths scheme also retained. Both assessment sessions were video recorded and discussed with Amy.

Figure 7.7

SECTION 8

Curriculum co-ordination

Subject co-ordinators often appear to face a daunting task in monitoring their subject throughout a school. In some schools this may require monitoring across four key stages, with a broad knowledge of the content requirement which this entails, and an expectation that co-ordinators will keep up to date with all changes in their particular subject. In many primary and special schools with a small number of staff, teachers will carry responsibility for several subjects, thus multiplying the difficulties of maintaining a monitoring brief. To add to this seemingly impossible venture, the majority of subject co-ordinators, whilst being aware of the advantages of classroom observation or co-operative teaching as part of the monitoring process, have little or no non-contact time within which to manoeuvre.

In an ideal world, subject co-ordinators would spend time in classrooms observing how their subject was being delivered. They would pass on their expertise through team teaching, and would have time to discuss their subject with teachers. They would provide assistance with planning and the development of teaching materials, and would still have time left over to co-ordinate resources. In the real world, co-ordinators are working with minimal time, have responsibilities for several aspects of school life, and seldom have time to monitor what is happening in their subject. The Office for Standards in Education (Ofsted) have made it clear that they consider arrangements for curriculum co-ordination and continuity to be an important issue (*Guidance on the Inspection of Special Schools,* 1995). Advice on how teachers, already over stretched by the demands of recent legislation can fulfil this responsibility has, however, been noticeable for its absence.

The section will begin from the standpoint that teachers, whilst recognising the importance of curriculum co-ordination, have only a limited amount of time within which to fulfil this role. In so doing, a model will be presented which attempts to meet the requirements of curriculum co-ordination through practical tasks designed to gain information and promote curriculum development. As with other sections of this book, sheets which may be freely photocopied are provided for teachers who wish to use or further develop the approach described.

What is the purpose of subject monitoring?

In many special and primary schools, staff are required to have a generic expertise which would be regarded as preposterous in secondary schools. Prior to the introduction of the National Curriculum, teachers taught a range of subjects, often working with only limited expertise in some of these. The prescriptive content of the National Curriculum has increased the pressure upon teachers to have a more in depth knowledge of the subjects which they are teaching. In many instances, this has coincided with a reduction in the number of local authority advisory staff available to provide the necessary training and support which would have allowed for a more logical transition through this period of change. All too often, teachers have been left feeling isolated in their efforts to increase their expertise in a number of subjects and across several key stages. To expect teachers to continue working within a generic framework with little support is unacceptable. An early role for the subject co-ordinator must therefore be to establish credibility and expertise in a subject and to become prepared to pass their knowledge on to colleagues in the school (Sebba, 1994). The role of subject co-ordinator as a support for colleagues is of paramount importance, and needs to be carefully thought out if it is to be effective.

In assuming a subject co-ordination role, it is equally important to recognise that other staff have a responsibility in supporting the co-ordinator (see section 3). Subject co-ordinators can have a tremendous and beneficial effect upon their subject in the school but, without the co-operation of all staff, and the support of the management of the school, many of the benefits are unlikely to be achieved. Having appointed co-ordinators, the managers and governors of the school have a duty to provide them with support in fulfilling their role. There should also be an obligation upon all staff to provide the information and co-operation necessary to enable co-ordinators to perform effectively.

Monitoring should be used as a means of supporting staff in curriculum delivery. It should ensure that pupils receive the broad, balanced, relevant and well differentiated curriculum which has become the alleged gospel of education in recent years. Monitoring must ask questions about curriculum coverage, pupil achievements and quality of teaching and provide opportunities for the non-specialist teacher to gain confidence and develop the skills which will enable them to teach subjects more effectively. It should also provide indicators for the co-ordinator of areas which require further development or adjustments to resourcing. Monitoring should be a collaborative process in which staff are fully involved with the co-ordinator in making decisions about adjustments to teaching or ways in which the curriculum may move forward.

Monitoring – I just don't have the time!

How, then, can the subject co-ordinator with minimal time be effective in monitoring the curriculum? Accepting that there is no real substitute for spending time in every class observing teachers, but that this may be impossible in practical terms, we must look for approaches which will gather information consistently, and achieve a balanced and manageable approach.

Tangible evidence related to the effectiveness of subject management and delivery can be obtained through a range of sources which can be examined outside the classroom. These include:

- teacher plans
- teacher records
- pupil's work
- reports.

In order to be effective in gathering information, it is essential that subject co-ordinators are clear about what they are seeking, and know where the answers are likely to be found. The grid provided in Figure 8:1 gives a list of key questions which co-ordinators may wish to ask about their subject, and indicates where some of the answers are likely to be found.

All of the evidence gained through this approach comes from documentary materials which can be examined at a time which is of greatest convenience to the co-ordinator and the class teacher. The grid does not provide an exhaustive list of questions, but rather gives an indication of some of the enquiries which a co-ordinator may make, and the sources of information which may be used to provide answers. Subject co-ordinators will wish to add to or subtract from this list, depending on the current position of their school, and of their subject.

Examination of documentary evidence is not sufficient in itself as a way of monitoring a subject. Other strategies need to be deployed which provide a systematic way of asking questions, interpreting information and taking action to move a subject forwards. Building upon the grid provided in Figure 8:1, one means of developing subject co-ordination is through the use of what may be termed a curriculum monitoring diary approach.

Using a curriculum monitoring diary

Any examination of curriculum documentation or pupil's work needs to be systematic and manageable. The use of a curriculum monitoring diary is one approach which assists with this task.

Figures 8:2 and 8:3 provide an example of a format which can be used as a subject monitoring diary. The format provided here is simple, and demands that comments are kept short and focused. After completion, the diary should be used as the basis for discussion and review with the class teacher, and as an indicator for any action to be taken. A particularly positive approach would be for the co-ordinator to complete the diary with the class teacher should time allow. In reality it is more likely that the subject co-ordinator will undertake this task alone.

The diary is used in the following way. The teacher examines documentary materials from a class, as indicated in Figure 8:1, asking the questions and using the information obtained to complete the diary. In practical terms, the subject co-ordinator should not expect to see the work and records of every pupil in the class, but should consider establishing a curriculum monitoring rota (see Figures 8:8 and 8:9), which will be explained in more detail later in this section. The curriculum diary collates information under four headings:

- work undertaken during the term
- pupil's work seen
- teacher records seen
- work planned for next term.

The boxes under these headings should be completed by the subject co-ordinator on the basis of the information gained from the documentary evidence.

After completion, this diary sheet should be used as the basis for discussion with the class teacher. Time is a valuable commodity, and many teachers feel that too much of it is spent in meetings. It is therefore essential that any meeting arranged between a subject co-ordinator and the class teacher is used to maximum effect. Co-ordinators should arrange a time of mutual convenience with the teacher to discuss the findings collated on the monitoring diary sheet, and to identify means of moving the subject forward. Figures 8:4 and 8:5 provide an example of a curriculum monitoring interview sheet which can help with this process. This sheet identifies areas to be discussed under five headings:

- planning and differentiation
- assessment, recording and reporting
- curriculum content
- resources
- INSET requirements.

It is completed on the basis of information gained and entered on the monitoring diary sheet and identifies clearly the date and time of a meeting which has been mutually agreed and the issues which the subject co-ordinator wishes to discuss with the class teacher. It should be given to the class teacher, along with a copy of the monitoring diary sheet, in advance of the meeting, giving sufficient time for the class teacher to identify any issues or questions which she may wish to discuss.

During the meeting between the subject co-ordinator and the class teacher, the curriculum monitoring diary should form the basis of much of the discussion. It should not, however, preclude opportunities for the class teacher to raise other matters related to the subject. This meeting may also be used as an opportunity to introduce new resources or curriculum materials, and to discuss the needs of individual pupils.

The frequency of this process may vary according to the size of the school and the time available to staff. Where a subject co-ordinator is managing several subjects, it may be that the monitoring for a specific subject cannot be carried out termly. There should, however, be an intention to conduct the monitoring process at least every other term to ensure that good practices are being maintained and that identified difficulties are being addressed. Ideally, the use of the monitoring diary and interview approach would be carried out termly in order that work from a greater number of pupils within each class could be examined.

Following the initial meeting, and those held in subsequent terms, information should be retained which will inform an annual report on the subject relating to the work of that class (see Figures 8:6 and 8:7). In the example provided here, the subject co-ordinator has reported under six headings:

- content and coverage
- pupil progress
- planning
- assessment, recording and reporting
- resources
- action to be taken.

This report should provide an indication of the status of the subject in the class at the time of writing. The content of the report should be agreed between the subject co-ordinator and the class teacher. The action to be taken should be considered in relation to needs in the subject elsewhere in the school and should be given a clear timetable.

As was stated earlier in this section, it would be unreasonable to expect a subject co-ordinator to examine the work of every pupil in every class through the monitoring diary process. Much will depend upon the time which the co-ordinator is able to give to this process, and the support which can be given by the management of the school. The process of selecting which pupil's work and records will be monitored should be a matter for agreement with the class teacher. It is essential, however, that a reasonable cross section of pupils is monitored each year. It may, for example, be advisable to sample a selection of three or four pupils who have very different needs. This would enable the subject co-ordinator to ask questions about differentiation and planning for a range of needs and should reveal evidence of how this is being achieved. Once the monitoring of work and records has been completed, the subject co-ordinator will need to record which pupils have been through this process and what was found. Figure 8:8 gives an example of a monitoring rota completed after the first term of this process. Figure 8:9 gives a blank version.

The curriculum monitoring diary approach as has been described, is illustrated in Figure 8:10. As stated earlier in this section, there is no real substitute for subject co-ordinators getting into class for observation and collaborative work. This system here described does not preclude the use of such approaches but should be seen as complementary to, and supportive of, any practical work which the subject co-ordinator can undertake in class.

It is helpful to be clear about the information to be obtained, to identify specific questions, and to know where the answers are likely to be found. The following grid provides one example which may be helpful

QUESTIONS	SOURCES OF INFORMATION
KEY: P.W.=Pupil's work, T.R.=Teacher records, T.P.=Teacher plans, R=Reports	
Is curriculum balance being achieved? Are pupils receiving their entitlement to all parts of the subject?	**P.W., T.R., T.P., R.**
Are teachers recording pupil achievements and experiences?	**T.R.**
Is work being differentiated to meet the individual needs of pupils?	**T.P., T.R.**
Are teachers using a range of teaching approaches?	**T.P.**
Are requirements for reporting the subject being met?	**R.**
Is there continuity between classes in each key stage?	**T.R., T.P.**
Is there progression in planning and delivery through the key stages?	**T.P., T.R.**
How good is teacher understanding of the subject?	**T.P., P.W.**
Are teachers using appropriate resources for curriculum delivery?	**T.P.**
Are teachers consistent in their judgements about pupil progress?	**P.W., T.R.**
Are targets set through annual review being addressed and met?	**P.W., T.R., T.P., R.**

Figure 8.1

CURRICULUM MONITORING DIARY TERM **Summer 1995**
CLASS **5 (KS2)** TEACHER **Miss Willis** SUBJECT **Art**

WORK UNDERTAKEN DURING THE TERM

Investigating and making
Still life drawing and painting of artefacts from history study unit on the Romans.

Mosaic collages of Roman floors

Fabric printing – Roman designs on cotton for ceremonial togas.

Pottery – Roman pots with scraffito designs.

Knowledge and understanding
Visit to museum to see the work of Roman potters.

PUPIL'S WORK SEEN

John Parsons: Drawings of Roman spear and sword in pencil, and other sketches in charcoal.

Elizabeth Carr: Coil pots with scrafitto design. Collage made with three other pupils.

Wasim Khan: Drawings in pencil of Roman helmet, and paintings of sword and spear.

TEACHER RECORDS SEEN

Records indicate all pupils receiving appropriate coverage through term's work.

Skills identified as focus during term – observation, choice and use of colours, and manipulative skills.

Observational drawing building upon work on buildings from last term. Miss Willis is using pupil sketchbooks as part of record, and has retained samples of pupil's work. All work retained is dated, and annotated.

WORK PLANNED FOR NEXT TERM

All pupils move up to Mr Evans and will do a textiles course next term. Class split into two groups, one group to complete course each half term.

Work planned – spinning and weaving with wool, using vegetable dyes for wool, tie dying, introduction to wax resist (batik).

Visit arranged to craft centre to see spinners, weavers and dyers at work. Spinning and weaving equipment on loan from county resource centre. Advisory teacher visiting twice (once for each group).

Figure 8.2

CURRICULUM MONITORING DIARY   TERM
CLASS   TEACHER   SUBJECT

WORK UNDERTAKEN DURING THE TERM

PUPIL'S WORK SEEN

TEACHER RECORDS SEEN

WORK PLANNED FOR NEXT TERM

Figure 8.3

CURRICULUM MONITORING INTERVIEW		
SUBJECT Science	**DATE** 18.2.96	**CLASS** 4

As agreed, the monitoring interview for your class will take place on Weds. March 4th at 4.00 p.m. During the meeting I would like to discuss some of the following ideas with you.

PLANNING AND DIFFERENTIATION
How is the new planning system going? Is it helping with planning for next term?
Can we look at planning for better inclusion of George in practical lessons?

ASSESSMENT, RECORDING AND REPORTING
Can we consider the requirements for the subject report to parents at the end of the summer term?

CURRICULUM CONTENT
Look together at the electricity and magnetism module to be taught next term. Any modifications needed to this term's module on animal homes?

RESOURCES
Were resources adequate for this term? Are there additional requirements for next term?
I would also like to show you some new software for the CD which has arrived and may be useful next term.

INSET REQUIREMENTS
Are you happy with the content of the three modules to be taught next year?
Do you need any training related to these, or to other science matters?

If you wish to discuss other matters, or particular pupils, or if you would like to see any specific materials or equipment related to the subject, could you please let me know as soon as possible. Thanks for your help.

Figure 8.4

CURRICULUM MONITORING INTERVIEW		
SUBJECT	**DATE**	**CLASS**

As agreed, the monitoring interview for your class will take place on ————————————at————
During the meeting I would like to discuss some of the following ideas with you.

PLANNING AND DIFFERENTIATION

ASSESSMENT, RECORDING AND REPORTING

CURRICULUM CONTENT

RESOURCES

INSET REQUIREMENTS

If you wish to discuss other matters, or particular pupils, or if you would like to see any specific materials or equipment related to the subject, could you please let me know as soon as possible. Thanks for your help.

Figure 8.5

ANNUAL SUBJECT MONITORING REPORT

SUBJECT Science **CLASS** 7 **DATE** July 1995

TEACHER John Phillips

CONTENT AND COVERAGE:
Three modules this year: Our Bodies, Change, and Moving Parts. Coverage of P.O.S. from three ATs. Coverage of investigative science built into modules. Pupils also completed a science skills course, learning how to use various pieces of science apparatus. Visit made to car factory as part of Moving Parts module.

PUPIL PROGRESS:
Teacher records show that most pupils made good progress through the year. Introduction of skills sessions appear to have improved pupil's performances in investigations. Consistent use of Makaton symbol program on P.C. has enabled Michael to take a more active part in written parts of lessons. Some pupils found the materials prepared for Change module very difficult, insufficient differentiation caused problems and exclusion of some.

PLANNING:
Planning improved in second half of year when approaches to differentiation were better established. Most planning now takes account of cross-curricular opportunities. We now need to concentrate on planning to ensure a wider range of teacher approaches.

ASSESSMENT, RECORDING AND REPORTING:
Assessment carried out at the end of each module. Tasks devised did not take enough account of providing access for Michael. Assessment tended to look largely at skills and knowledge, and not at application. Need to incorporate assessment into investigative approaches. New recording system is being consistently applied, and contributed well to end of year report.

RESOURCES:
Need to review resources for Change module. More books related to moving parts, particularly those with less text, would be useful.

ACTION TO BE TAKEN:
Review assessment procedures for pupils with special needs. Investigate resource needs. Consider a wider range of pupil self evaluation methods – work with Jenny from class 4, and Clare from class 5 on this as they have similar concerns.

Figure 8.6

ANNUAL SUBJECT MONITORING REPORT

SUBJECT **CLASS** **DATE**

TEACHER

CONTENT AND COVERAGE:

PUPIL PROGRESS:

PLANNING:

ASSESSMENT, RECORDING AND REPORTING:

RESOURCES:

ACTION TO BE TAKEN:

Figure 8.7

SUBJECT MONITORING ROTA MATHEMATICS

CLASS 4   YEAR 1995/96   TEACHER Clive King

	AUTUMN			SPRING			SUMMER		
PUPIL'S NAME	Paul Sutton	Ryan Clarke	Sue Longford	Wendy Bush	Zaheer Hussein	Leisa Watts	Clare Wilson	Jacob Cohen	Nick Parks
PUPIL'S WORK	Checked 12/12/95 Work on ATs 2 & 3 Marked to date	Checked 12/12/95 All work on AT2 Marked to date	Checked 12/12/95 Work on ATs 2 & 3 Marked to date						
TEACHER RECORDS	Checked 15/12/95	Checked 12/12/95	Checked 15/12/95 No records for AT1						
TEACHER PLANS	Emphasis next term on ATs 3 & 4	Additional support to be provided by SEN co-ordinator on Tues.	Continuing work on AT 2						
REPORTS	None this term	Report prepared for SEN review in Jan. Sent to parents	None this term						

ANNUAL MEETING WITH TEACHER   DATE   17/1/96
Comments
Discussed the need to give some attention to AT1, and agreed to provide some ideas for second half of spring term. Good level of support being provided for Ryan, some extra help to be provided on Tuesdays by Sue Robbins. New GINN workbooks appear popular, need to review availability of resources for AT4, and to ensure that Clive is familiar with range of software for data handling in summer term.

Figure 8.8

SUBJECT MONITORING ROTA **MATHEMATICS**

CLASS 4   YEAR   TEACHER

	AUTUMN			SPRING			SUMMER		
PUPIL'S NAME									
PUPIL'S WORK									
TEACHER RECORDS									
TEACHER PLANS									
REPORTS									

ANNUAL MEETING WITH TEACHER DATE
Comments

Figure 8.9

CURRICULUM MONITORING
THE APPROACH DESCRIBED IN THIS SECTION

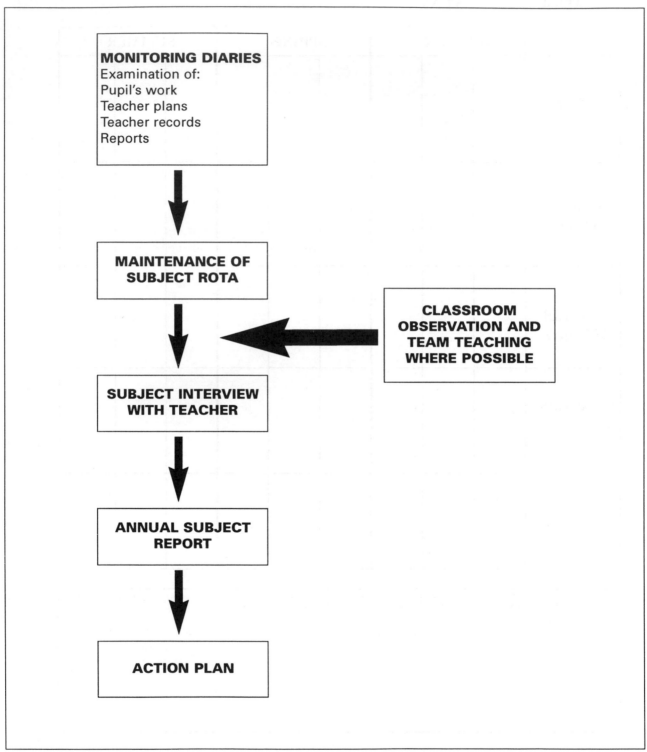

MONITORING DIARIES
Examination of:
Pupil's work
Teacher plans
Teacher records
Reports

MAINTENANCE OF SUBJECT ROTA

CLASSROOM OBSERVATION AND TEAM TEACHING WHERE POSSIBLE

SUBJECT INTERVIEW WITH TEACHER

ANNUAL SUBJECT REPORT

ACTION PLAN

Figure 8.10

SECTION 9

Meeting the challenge

'If you'd said to me a few years ago that I'd ever be teaching *Romeo and Juliet* or *Julius Caesar* to my kids, I'd have laughed. I mean, for English we'd mainly been worrying about whether they could fill in an application form or read the destination board on a bus. But now that I'm doing Shakespeare, I wouldn't stop. It's shown us what the kids can do if you give them the chance. And there's so much in it for them – not just the language and the heritage stuff, but real, relevant ideas. It gets us into discussions that are about their lives as well as about Shakespeare's characters – about families and difficulties with your parents and about power and corruption – great ways into a lot of the material we need to cover for the older students in personal and social education. So, yes, this is one bit of the National Curriculum I'd want to hang on to – it's been brilliant.'

When the National Curriculum was first introduced, there was a considerable amount of debate about whether its influence should be seen as positive or negative (Sebba and Fergusson, 1991; Sebba and Byers, 1992). It has been our contention in this book that the National Curriculum has become firmly established as a significant but not all-encompassing part of the framework of the whole curriculum for all schools. Many teachers, like the English co-ordinator in a school for pupils with moderate learning difficulties we cite above, have positive things to say about the efforts they have made to provide access for their pupils to a curriculum which is now seen as an entitlement. It is encouraging, for instance, to debate the development of sex education programmes within the science and health education schemes of work in schools for pupils with profound and multiple learning difficulties or to observe classes of pupils with severe learning difficulties participating meaningfully in highly successful and clearly enjoyable modern foreign language lessons. Again and again, teachers who have approached the challenge of access to the National Curriculum honestly and imaginatively say that, despite their doubts and misgivings, they now set great store by classroom activities which they might otherwise not have dreamed of attempting.

These initiatives are not perceived as successful because they are part of the National Curriculum, or because school inspectors seek to grade them as evidence of school effectiveness, or even because local employers feel that they make the workforce more efficient. So what is the nature of the enthusiasm which is tangible among many teachers working with pupils with special educational needs? Why, in spite of the enormity of the workload and the frustrations over shifts and turns in policy, have many teachers decided that the National Curriculum is, in many ways, a force for liberation and emancipation rather than the restrictive influence that was once feared?

School autonomy

We have argued, in section 1 of this book, that the National Curriculum can no longer be characterised as an overbearing and unwelcome invader upon curriculum development territory, pushing aside other indigenous priorities. The National Curriculum has been trimmed down to a size where it can be adopted as part of the framework of the whole curriculum without jeopardising the well-being of other aspects of school life, as we emphasise in section 2. Schools' own priorities, whether these are revealed in physiotherapy sessions or canoeing trips to Wales, are to be seen as an important expression of the unique characteristics of different school communities. Schools are encouraged to develop their own curricula around the statutory foundations and to make them individual in terms of content and structure by linking them firmly to the needs of the school's pupils.

We believe that it is appropriate for school communities to take this opportunity for autonomy very seriously. As we have argued before (Byers and Rose, 1994), schools should be making their own decisions within the parameters of a properly constituted common framework. Part of the spirit of enthusiasm we report is due, we believe, to a resurgence of self confidence in schools – a sense that it is possible for schools to return to defining, to a large extent, their own agendas for development. One of the useful outcomes of the system of school inspection is that schools themselves can use the criteria (Ofsted, 1995), alongside other strategies, as a tool for self review. As section 3 argues, the planning cycle, which moves from policy making, through implementation towards review and revision, should be defined and managed by school communities. The school that sets its own agenda; its own targets; its own criteria for judging progress, and its own pace of change, is in accord with the spirit of the times and will reap its own rewards. Among these rewards, we would argue, is the sense of common purpose which comes with shared endeavour, joint responsibility, co-operative ownership and team work. As we have emphasised, developments which are driven by pressure from the heavy hand of management, wielding the threat of external accountability, will be superficial, short term and ineffective. A collegiate approach, characterised by clarity of intent, consensus and a fair and reasonable workload for all, is much more likely to bring about deep and long lasting progress which is of real benefit to the whole school community.

It is one of the central contentions of this book that this is the best way to work – indeed, that many stages in curriculum planning *require* collaboration at various levels in order to be meaningful. The task of negotiating breadth and balance within the whole curriculum (see sections 2 and 3) should involve the widest possible representation from the whole school community – staff, governors, parents, pupils and other professionals. The development of units of work should be conducted at a departmental or key stage team level, with the input of subject co-ordinators in a supporting role (see sections 4 and 5). Information collected by individual subject co-ordinators in auditing and monitoring their subject at different levels needs to be considered in a wider forum (see section 8). Many schools have created departmental or key stage teams who, in addition to their responsibility for developing schemes of work, consider and act upon issues raised through review and evaluation. As the *Code of Practice* (DfE, 1994) suggests, even short term target setting can be enhanced where class teachers or pastoral tutors work closely with pupils, colleagues and parents (see section 7).

Another major theme of this book is that curriculum planning is a phased development task which takes time and never reaches a 'finished' state. It leads rather to a continuous cycle of review and development which, in close relation to the staff development plan and within the school development plan, is steered by the whole school curriculum development plan.

Changing practice   Curriculum development can never be reduced to a paper exercise, however.

Although much of this book describes a process of documenting innovation, we would assert that writing up schemes of work is meaningless unless changes in policy and documentation are reflected in revitalised classroom processes. In opening this chapter with the enthusiastic words of a teacher, we mean to celebrate the expertise that exists; to emphasise that innovation is driving positive change, and to encourage schools to focus their efforts on offering pupils better teaching and improved learning opportunities. The countless wheelbarrow loads of slick documentation which are carted away for pre-inspection analysis are worth nothing if practice at the interface between teachers and learners does not move forward.

Of course, practice is moving forwards – and this is the main reason why we have been motivated to collect together some examples of ways in which schools set their work down on paper. Improving practice is also the major motivating force which drives schools to continue to devote time, energy, commitment and enthusiasm to curriculum development work at a time when experience might have led to demoralisation. Teachers value the sorts of developments we have described above because they touch the lives of pupils in relevant, purposeful ways. Returning to the illustrations we gave earlier in this section, it is important for all young people to have an awareness of their bodies and their sexual selves, just as learning about culture and communication in France means a great deal to young people who may go there on holiday and who are aware that their brothers and sisters study the same language in their schools.

Entitlement to content

The recognition that pupils with special educational needs have an entitlement to content of this sort is, in itself, important. In many instances, the National Curriculum has encouraged schools to look beyond a narrow, utilitarian curriculum and has opened up new horizons in terms of the skills, knowledge, understanding and experience which might be offered to pupils with special educational needs of all kinds. We are firmly convinced that the re-evaluation and review which has gone on with regard to the curriculum for pupils with special educational needs in recent years has been timely and productive and that it should continue. The programmes of study for the subjects of the National Curriculum, together with religious education and the cross-curricular elements, have broadened the curriculum provided for pupils with special educational needs. As we noted in section 1, important modifications made in the interests of the special educational needs lobby helped to shape the Dearing review of the National Curriculum. Responsibility for managing balance in the whole curriculum is now firmly located in schools. It is an appropriate sense of balance, tempered by a clear sense of relevance in the light of pupils' needs and best interests, which makes entitlement to breadth a liberating possibility rather than a looming threat of overload.

Flexibility of access

The structural changes in the revised National Curriculum are hugely significant. The freedom which schools have to move around within the programmes of study, treating some aspects in depth and others in outline while selecting material which is developmentally appropriate from among the key stages, represents a great gain. The routes to access are now open although this does not diminish the task of making that access a practical reality. Extending access and probing the programmes of study for further areas which can be meaningfully taught to wider groups of pupils will present an ongoing challenge. As we have sought to demonstrate in this book, many schools are engaged in this process, revitalised by the knowledge that decisions about modes and levels of access are properly taken within school communities.

Part of this discretion is exercised in finding school specific solutions to the challenge of curriculum design and management. In many places through this book we have presented alternative, equally valid, ways of moving forward. Whether schools choose to proceed with long term plans for units of work, with modules, or with integrated schemes of work, pupils hopefully experience a variety of approaches to teaching. For them, the increase in exploration, problem solving and active enquiry which accompanies wholehearted attempts to implement the National Curriculum brings new opportunities to learn how to learn. This book has looked briefly at some of the issues arising from co-operative group work, or from pupil involvement in review and evaluation. We hope that initiatives like these, which bring another perspective regarding balance and variety to the classroom, will continue and prosper.

Inclusion

As all of the above suggests, we would argue that a curriculum for all, emphasising inclusion rather than separation, is a practical possibility. Many of the examples of good practice which we have cited in these pages have cross-phase implications and can be applied in a wide range of situations. This is not to argue simply for locational inclusion. There are pupils with special educational needs attending mainstream schools who find themselves marginalised and patronised, given the role of observer on the periphery of activity, rarely participants at the heart of what is going on. At the same time, staff in special schools are breaking down separatist streaming structures and focusing upon curriculum development initiatives which emphasise differentiation, access for all and inclusion. We value the work of such schools very highly and hope that their example in developing an inclusive curriculum will inform strategic planning towards structures which give meaningful expression to locational inclusion.

Concluding remarks

We are convinced that the National Curriculum has, in many senses, been a positive influence and a force for liberation and emancipation for pupils with special educational needs and their staff alike. We do not underestimate the enormity of the tasks which all schools have faced. However, although the time scale for innovation has been hectic and the messages often confused, we suggest that an opportunity for assimilation, consolidation and steady progress has arrived. Models for development, which have emerged painfully and uncertainly under the pressure of torrents of legislation, can be applied with more confidence and dignity to new subjects or to other aspects of the curriculum. Working with less haste will mean that more attention can be paid to the quality of innovation. As we have stressed, a phased programme of development will, over time, encompass the review and evaluation of policy and practice.

We are grateful to all the schools whose work is represented in these pages and hope that this book contributes to a growing sense of self confidence in other school communities, founded upon purposeful curriculum planning.

Bibliography

Ainscow, M. (1989) 'How should we respond to individual needs?', in Ainscow, M. and Florek, A. (eds) *Special Educational Needs: towards a whole school approach.* London: Fulton.

Alexander, R., Rose, J. and Woodhead, C. (1992) *Curriculum Organisation and Classroom Practice in Primary Schools.* London: HMSO.

Ashdown, R., Carpenter, B. and Bovair, K. (1991) 'The Curriculum Challenge', in Ashdown, R., Carpenter, B. and Bovair, K. (eds) *The Curriculum Challenge.* London: Falmer.

Byers, R. (1992) 'Topics: from myths to objectives', in Bovair, K., Carpenter, B. and Upton, G. (eds) *Special Curricula Needs.* London: Fulton.

Byers, R. (1994a) 'Providing opportunities for effective learning', in Rose, R., Fergusson, A., Coles, C., Byers, R. and Banes, D. (eds) *Implementing the Whole Curriculum for Pupils with Learning Difficulties.* London: Fulton.

Byers, R. (1994b) 'Teaching as dialogue: teaching approaches and learning styles in schools for pupils with learning difficulties', in Coupe-O'Kane, J. and Smith, B. (eds) *Taking Control: enabling pupils with learning difficulties.* London: Fulton.

Byers, R. and Rose, R. (1994) 'Schools should decide . . .', in Rose, R., Fergusson, A., Coles, C., Byers, R. and Banes, D. (eds) *Implementing the Whole Curriculum for Pupils with Learning Difficulties.* London: Fulton.

Carpenter, B. (1992) 'The Whole Curriculum: meeting the needs of the whole child', in Bovair, K., Carpenter, B. and Upton, G. (eds) *Special Curricula Needs.* London: Fulton.

Charlton, T. and David, K. (1989) *Managing Behaviour.* Basingstoke: Macmillan.

Chesworth, S. (1994) 'Devising and implementing a cross-curricular school recording system', in Rose, R., Fergusson, A., Coles, C., Byers, R. and Banes, D. (eds) *Implementing the Whole Curriculum for Pupils with Learning Difficulties.* London: Fulton.

Dearing, Sir R. (1993a) *The National Curriculum and its Assessment – an interim report.* York/London: NCC/SEAC.

Dearing, Sir R. (1993b) *The National Curriculum and its Assessment – final report.* London: SCAA.

Department for Education (1993) *Education Act 1993.* London: HMSO.

Department for Education (1994) *Code of Practice on the Identification and Assessment of Special Educational Needs.* London: DfE.

Department for Education (1995) *The National Curriculum.* London: HMSO.

Fergusson, A. (1994) 'Planning for communication', in Rose, R., Fergusson, A., Coles, C., Byers, R. and Banes, D. (eds) *Implementing the Whole Curriculum for Pupils with Learning Difficulties.* London: Fulton.

Galloway, S. and Banes, D. (1994) 'Beyond the simple audit', in Rose, R., Fergusson, A., Coles, C., Byers, R. and Banes, D. (eds) *Implementing the Whole Curriculum for Pupils with Learning Difficulties.* London: Fulton.

Galton, M. (1989) *Teaching in the Primary School.* London: Fulton.

Griffiths, M. (1994) *Transition to Adulthood – the role of education for young people with severe learning difficulties.* London: Fulton.

Hardwick, J. and Rushton, P. (1994) 'Pupil participation in their own records of achievement', in Rose, R., Fergusson, A., Coles, C., Byers, R. and Banes, D. (eds) *Implementing the Whole Curriculum for Pupils with Learning Difficulties.* London: Fulton.

Hargreaves, D. and Hopkins, D. (1991), *The Empowered School.* London: Cassell.

Hart, S. (1992) 'Differentiation – way forward or retreat?'. *British Journal of Special Education.* 19, (1), 10–12.

Johnson, R.T., and Johnson, D.W. (1983) 'Effects of cooperative, competitive and individualistic learning experiences on social development'. *Exceptional Children.* 49, (4), 323-329.

Lawson, H. (1992) *Practical Record Keeping for Special Schools.* London: Fulton.

Lewis, A. (1992) 'From planning to practice', *British Journal of Special Education,* 19, (1), 24–27.

MacNamara, S. and Rose, R. (1995) 'Children's management of their own learning – the QUEST project', paper presented at the *International Special Education Congress:* Birmingham.

McCall, C. (1983), *Classroom Grouping for Special Need.* Stratford-upon-Avon: National Council for Special Education.

National Curriculum Council (1990) *Curriculum Guidance 3: The Whole Curriculum.* York: NCC.

National Curriculum Council (1992) *Curriculum Guidance 9: The National Curriculum and Pupils with Severe Learning Difficulties.* York: NCC.

National Curriculum Council (1993) *Planning the National Curriculum at Key Stage 2.* York : NCC.

Nind, M. and Hewett, D. (1994) *Access to Communication*. London: Fulton.

OFSTED (1993) *Curriculum Organisation and Classroom Practice in Primary Schools – a follow up report*. London: HMSO.

OFSTED (1995) *Guidance on the Inspection of Special Schools*. London: HMSO.

Ouvry, C. (1991) 'Access for Pupils with Profound and Multiple Learning Difficulties', in Ashdown, R., Carpenter, B. and Bovair, K. (eds) *The Curriculum Challenge*. London: Falmer.

Preedy, M. (1992), *Managing the Effective School*. London. PCP.

Reid, K., Hopkins, D. and Holly, P. (1987) *Towards the Effective School*. Oxford. Blackwell.

Rose, R. (1991) 'A jigsaw approach to group work', *British Journal of Special Education*, 18, (2), 54–57.

Rose, R. (1994), 'A modular approach to the curriculum for pupils with learning difficulties', in Rose, R., Fergusson, A., Coles, C., Byers, R. and Banes, D. (eds) *Implementing the Whole Curriculum For Pupils with Learning Difficulties*. London: Fulton.

Rose, R., Fergusson, A., Coles, C., Byers, R. and Banes, D. (eds) (1994) *Implementing the Whole Curriculum for Pupils with Learning Difficulties*. London: Fulton.

Rouse, M. (1991) 'Assessment, the National Curriculum and Special Educational Needs: confusion or consensus?', in Ashdown, R., Carpenter, B. and Bovair, K. (eds) *The Curriculum Challenge*. London: Falmer.

SCAA (1994) *Consultation on the National Curriculum – an Introduction*. London: SCAA.

SCAA (1995) *Planning the Curriculum at Key Stages 1 and 2*. London: SCAA.

Scott, L. (1994) *On the Agenda – sex education for young people with learning difficulties*. London: Image in Action.

Sebba, J. (1994) *History for All*. London: Fulton.

Sebba, J. and Byers, R. (1992) 'The National Curriculum: control or liberation for pupils with learning difficulties?' *The Curriculum Journal*. 3, (2), 143–160.

Sebba, J. and Fergusson, A. (1991) 'Reducing the marginalisation of pupils with severe learning difficulties through curricular initiatives', in Ainscow, M. (ed) *Effective Schools for All*. London: Fulton.

Sebba, J., Byers, R. and Rose, R. (1993) *Redefining the Whole Curriculum for Pupils with Learning Difficulties*. London: Fulton.

Slavin, R.E. (1988), 'Cooperative learning and student achievement'. *Educational Leadership*. 46, (2), 31-33.

Southworth, G. (1993) 'School leadership and school development: reflections from research'. *School Organization*. 13, (1), 73–87.

Stevens, C. (1995) 'News from SCAA', *British Journal of Special Education*. 22, (1), 30-31.

Swing, S.R., and Peterson, P.L. (1982) 'The relationship of student ability and small group interaction to student achievement'. *American Education Research Journal*. 19, (2), 259 - 274.

Tate, N. (1994) 'Target vision', *Times Educational Supplement*, 2 December 1994.

Tilstone, C. (1991) 'Pupils' Views', in Tilstone, C. (ed) *Teaching Pupils with Severe Learning Difficulties*. London: Fulton.

West-Burnham, J. (1994) 'Strategy, policy and planning' in Bush, T. and West-Burnham, J. (eds) *The Principles of Educational Management*. Harlow: Longman.

Widget Software (1994) *Writing with Symbols*. Leamington: Widget.